PELICAN BOOKS

FLATION
not INflation of prices
not DEflation of jobs

Abba P. Lerner is Professor of Economics at
Queens College. He has taught at the University
of California (Berkeley), the London School of
Economics, Columbia University, the University
of Kansas City, the University of Virginia, the
New School for Social Research, Amherst Col-
lege, Roosevelt University, and Michigan State
University. Major books to his credit include
*The Economics of Control, The Economics of
Employment, Essays in Economic Analysis,* and
Everybody's Business. Articles by Professor Lerner
have appeared in *Commentary, Midstream,
American Scholar, Encounter,* and numerous other
publications.

FLATION

not INflation of prices
not DEflation of jobs

Abba P. Lerner

*What You Always Wanted
to Know about Inflation,
Depression, and the Dollar*

Penguin Books Inc
Baltimore • Maryland

Penguin Books Inc
7110 Ambassador Road
Baltimore, Maryland 21207, U.S.A.

First published by Quadrangle Books, Inc., New York, 1972
Published in Pelican Books 1973
Reprinted 1974

Contents

Preface

THE term "flation" was first (and perhaps last) used, so far as I know, in an early James Stewart film, *Mr. Smith Goes to Washington;* a United States Senator declares himself to be in favor of "neither inflation nor deflation but flation." This must have been at about the time (1941) that I coined the term "functional finance" to describe a policy of having "neither too much spending nor too little spending" in the economy as a whole. "Functional finance" did go a little farther than "flation" in indicating the nature of the instruments that government could use in carrying out this policy, but functional finance suggests a complete symmetry between "too much spending" and "too little spending" even more than "flation" suggests symmetry between inflation and deflation of prices.

A major part of this book deals with the tragic consequences of policies based on the view that the inflation-deflation issue is a purely symmetrical matter of prices going up —inflation—when there is too much spending, and coming down—deflation—whenever there is too little spending. These policies, both here and abroad, consisted of treating inflation due to pressure by sellers (sellers' inflation) as if it were demand inflation (inflation due to too much spending). They treated it by holding down total spending in the economy. Unfortunately, this has little effect on the rising prices of sellers' inflation, but is very effective in deflating the economy—increasing unemployment and creating recession if not depression.

For the audience of the Senator in *Mr. Smith,* during the great depression of the 1930's, "deflation" inevitably suggested disastrous unemployment, although the depression was often confused with, or supposed to be caused by falling prices. But the effective appeal of "nor deflation" was in its being taken to mean "nor depression." The slogan of "neither inflation nor deflation but flation" was sufficiently ahead of its time for its wisdom to be seen only as wit.

Introduction to the Pelican Edition

In the year or so that has passed since this book was written, there have occurred a number of events that might have been mentioned if I were writing the book now, but these have not significantly affected its substance, which is the explanation of the economic forces and policies connected with inflation and depression, domestically and internationally. There will undoubtedly be further such developments before the Pelican edition appears in the bookstores, but these are no more likely than the earlier ones to affect the general principles with which this book is concerned.

It is, however, necessary to point out that the "Phase Three" of President Richard M. Nixon's New Economic Policy as announced in January 1973 is not the same as the Phase Three of this book. In the book Phase Three refers to a condition in which the regulation of wages and prices under Phase Two has completed its task of eliminating the upward pressure on wages and prices by labor and business, so that the regulation has become inoperative. In the announced "Phase Three" the wage and price regulation continues to be operative, with some minor changes in the manner of its administration. "Voluntary" restraints (reinforced by the threat of potential sanctions) replaced "mandatory" restraints (softened by possibilities of pressure and negotiation). The announced "Phase Three" is really a continuation of Phase Two, changed in little but the name. It remains to be seen whether the changes will increase or diminish effectiveness. If the rate of inflation, which had been reduced from 6 to $3\frac{1}{2}\%$ per annum, is stabilized at or below $3\frac{1}{2}\%$ (or perhaps even reduced to zero), we would have the real change that introduces what I called Phase Three. The fear of inflation will have abated, and a policy of "high full employment" will be in the cards. On the other hand, the change could result in an acceleration of inflation even while a promised tighter budgetary and monetary policy reverses the 1972 reduction in unemployment. Fortunately, the purpose of this book is not to provide the latest forecasts but to clarify the way things work, so that the reader can apply this understanding to the latest headlines.

A number of minor changes and corrections have been made for the Pelican edition, as well as a little updating. A paragraph has been added at the end of Chapter 14, and the end of Chapter 15 has been rewritten.

A. P. L.
February 5, 1973

Chapter 1

WHY IS THIS INFLATION
DIFFERENT FROM
ALL OTHER INFLATIONS?

INFLATION originally meant blowing air into a balloon. When the balloon was blown up it expanded. Filled with a gas lighter than air, it rose. And the children thought that was great fun. If the gas leaked out, the balloon deflated. It contracted, fell to the ground, and lost its beautiful shape. The children were very sad.

Applied to the world of business and economics, inflation came to mean a condition where the pressure of prices put a dangerous strain on the fabric of the economy, like a balloon blown up too far. Or it might mean a condition where prices were rising higher and higher, like a lighter-than-air balloon. The economy was then often declared to be "overheated" and fated to fall down to earth, like a fire balloon when the fuel is all gone. Or perhaps, like a hydrogen or helium balloon, it would rise very high, expanding farther and farther in the low pressure of the upper atmosphere until finally it burst and crashed. The fire-balloon analogy fits more closely the economic movements of business cycles in which "booms" with rising prices were followed by "busts" when prices fell; while the case of the hydrogen-helium balloon describes runaway or "galloping" inflations—the "hyperinflations" in which prices rose to hundreds, thousands, millions and even billions of times what they had been, and then there was an economic collapse.

When this happened in Germany in 1923, prices rose to more than ten billion times what they had been a year before. In the United States during the Civil War prices rose "only" by some 20,000 per cent. Life became uncomfortable. Production was disorganized. Many people were ruined, while some made enormous profits. Ultimately, nearly everybody suffered severely in the resulting chaos, when more and more people, instead of staying at their jobs, rushed to buy something, anything, before prices rose still further. Less and less was produced. There was a general impoverishment in real goods while everyone became a "millionaire" in the depreciated money.

The current inflationary condition in the United States is not hyperinflation, but what has come to be called creeping inflation. The rate of increase in prices grew in a few years from about 2 per cent a year to about 6 per cent a year. Such a rate of price increase does not by itself disrupt or disorganize the economy. It does not interfere with the efficient production and distribution of all the goods and services that we enjoy. Indeed, while the population has been growing steadily, the quantity of goods and services we are currently producing and consuming has also been increasing, not only in total but also in the amount available per person. It has not increased as much as could have been expected; indeed it increased much less than in a number of other countries. But it will become clear that this lagging was not a direct result of inflation.

This does not mean that such a "creeping" inflation does not matter. If prices rise at 6 per cent a year they would *double* in about eleven years. Prices would rise not 66 per cent, but about 100 percent because each year the 6 per cent rise will be compounded. In 22 years prices would have doubled twice. They would be four times what they are now. Anybody with a fixed income would be able to buy only half as much in eleven years and only a quarter as much in twenty-two years. Pensioners would be impoverished. They would have lost half or three quarters of their pensions in real terms—in purchasing power.

Even a moderate or creeping inflation is thus unquestionably bad. The evil is usually much exaggerated, but that does not stop it from being a bad thing. Since the essence of inflation is rising prices, it is bad for the buyers who have to pay the higher prices and who, therefore, are made poorer to that degree. But since there is always somebody who *receives* the higher price, the seller's gain must be balanced against the buyer's loss. Nevertheless, one often hears accounts of the evils of inflation as if there were only buyers and no sellers of goods and services.

A famous example, or perhaps I should say a notorious one, is the statement made by President Nixon in his State of the Nation message in 1970. He said that in the course of ten years the Government of the United States had incurred deficits amounting to $57-billion, which resulted in an inflation that raised the cost of living of the average American family of four by $200 a month. This amounts to about $600-billion* so that it appears to have brought about a *loss* to American families of more than ten times the taxes that would have covered the deficit and to continue to burden them to the extent of $120-billion a year—or more than twice the cumula-

---

* 50 million (families) times $100 (a month—the *average* increase over the 10 years) times 12 (months in a year) times 10 (years) equals $600-billion.

tive deficit over the 10 sinful years—a very bad business indeed. The President greatly regretted it and promised he would try to avoid it in the future. This argument disregards the corresponding *gain* to the sellers of the goods bought by the American families. These sellers had their incomes *increased* by the same $600-billion and will continue to earn the additional $120-billion per annum in the future.

The President's argument can simply be reversed. He could have patted himself and his predecessors on the back for having obtained such a great increase in incomes for the American public at the mere cost of $57-billion in deficits! This reversed argument is, of course, no better than the original one made by the President. The two arguments completely cancel each other out. Any proper accounting must consider both the higher payments and the higher receipts, which are the two sides of the same transactions. It is in the course of cancelling these out that we are brought up against the injustices that really make inflation objectionable.

Inflation is not as unpopular as one might judge it to be from the conventional exaggeration of its evils in public statements. While everybody grumbles about higher prices when he is buying, almost everybody is pleased, or at least relieved, when he is able to increase his profits by raising the price of what he sells, or to obtain higher wages for work or higher interest or dividends from investments. These are not merely the other side of the increased prices. They regularly come to *more* than the increase in prices.

This is certainly true in the long run. This century's standard of living—many times higher than in any previous century—is only a reflection of the far greater increase in incomes than in prices over the centuries. In the last thirty years prices have doubled in the United States, but total income has increased fourfold. Over-all we are as well off as if there had been no inflation at all and our income had been doubled, or as if our income had remained unchanged and prices had halved so that we could buy twice as much with each dollar. While inflation has been going on, we have been doing rather well. Some other countries have done much better, and some have not done as well as we have, but all countries have had some inflation and almost every country has at the same time had an increase in its real income, not only in total but also per capita of increasing population.

There is yet another and a stronger reason that the opposition to inflation was so weak that it permitted inflation to become the rule rather than the exception throughout history. The reason is that inflation has usually been observed together with the relatively more prosperous periods within the long term or secular growth in real income we have just considered.

Of course, there is a complicated argument as to whether prosperity was due to inflation or inflation was due to prosperity. We shall see that no very useful answer can be given to the question when it is put so simply. But there is indeed a connection between more spending and inflation, as well as a connection between more spending and prosperity. From this it is tempting to suppose that there is a causal connection between inflation and prosperity—that inflation *causes* prosperity—although this does *not* follow.

Inflation was often observed during economic booms, when there was high employment with high profits and generally improved conditions of life. The booms tended to be followed by periods of depression, bankruptcies, serious unemployment and greater poverty, and it was generally during such unpleasant periods that prices fell. The primary objection to inflation was, therefore, not on account of the actual evils of the inflation, its injustices against those with relatively fixed incomes. Rather there was the feeling that although inflation itself was pleasant, profitable and even exhilarating for most, it was only temporary and, therefore, "unsound." The enjoyment of the prosperity that accompanied inflation was viewed as a sin, which brought its punishment to society in the business losses, bankruptcies, unemployment and increased poverty that inevitably followed. But for the *individual* punishment was uncertain. This left the sin of inflation sufficiently attractive to enough people for them to promote or permit inflationary policies, despite their belief in a high probability of punishment by depression—that the boom would have to be followed by the bust.

The connection between inflation and prosperity, both in the long-term or secular context, as well as in the short-term context, is that while *adequate* spending is necessary for prosperity, *too much* spending causes inflation.

The excessive spending shows itself first of all, in higher prices. When buyers try to buy more than is available, prices will go up. But it is not enough to speak of this as if it were some physical or chemical reaction of prices to excessive spending (or to an excessive quantity of money, even if we are clear that the quantity of money is relevant only insofar as it results in excessive spending). We have to see how prices, which are arranged and agreed to by the buyers and the sellers, come to be raised.

Prices may be raised when buyers find that what they wanted to buy has already been sold out. They will then come to the stores earlier the next day. Some will even offer the sellers a higher price in order to get the item. Another way prices rise is when the sellers, or some of them, realize that they can ask for a higher price and still be able to sell all that they have available, they will raise prices before they have sold out all their supplies.

The first symptom of the excess demand that causes prices to rise will thus be the existence of unsatisfied potential customers when supplies have been exhausted. This can happen only if the customers have been trying to buy more than 100 per cent of what is available. The second symptom, not so easy to verify, is the buyers' raising the price offered, or the sellers' raising the price asked for, *in anticipation* of a shortage and of unsatisfied potential customers at the previous price.

In some cases the first symptom of excess demand—the empty shelves while customers are still clamoring to buy more—is quickly eliminated by an increase in the price. By discouraging buyers and encouraging suppliers, the price increase brings supply and demand into equilibrium and the only remaining symptom is the higher price. And if the amount of money spent on the item keeps on increasing, the price will keep on increasing too.

In other cases there are resistances and delays in the price increase. The sellers may be afraid of losing the goodwill of customers, or of government interference, or they may feel that the profits they make are already exorbitant and do not want to engage in what may be considered "profiteering" or "gouging."

In such cases many other symptoms of excess demand emerge. There are lines of customers trying to get some of the items before the store runs out of supplies. Stores cease to be clean and attractive. Advertising and salesmanship, such as attractive window displays, fall off. Store owners find it unnecessary to be polite or even considerate to their customers, to wrap their goods prettily or conveniently or to provide services that had been customary. A black market develops, where some of those who have managed to get supplies of the item resell it at a price higher than the store's. This phenomenon is well known in connection with the theater. Tickets obtained at official prices are resold to eager customers for much more. Suppliers begin to discriminate among customers in various ways; choosing the lucky ones to whom they will sell and the unlucky ones who will be told that there is none left. They sell to friends, rather than to those whom they do not like or against whom they have some prejudice. They will sell to their regular customers and to "good" customers and not to "poor" customers. They will try to make poor customers into good customers by getting them to buy something else together with the scarce item. They might not sell to strangers, but rudely tell them to go where they have been buying before—and this can work a hardship on new arrivals in town.

The reader who has lived through a period of excess demand will recognize these symptoms and will no doubt be able to think of many more of this kind. In a sense they sound anecdotal rather than systematic or scientific. These phenomena seem to be more in the province of the sociologist than of the economist and they are not easily converted into statistics and index numbers. Yet, they are essential to recognition of whether the excess demand, which is supposed to be the cause of the inflation, really exists.

Much of the failure of traditional economics to explain current problems, or to indicate how to deal with them, stems from the neglect of these phenomena, because they cannot easily be translated into statistics or fed into computers as numerical data. They are, nevertheless, well recognized in all descriptions of what happens during inflationary periods when it is clear that there is excess demand.

In the inflation of 1970–71 all these symptoms were absent.

Prices were rising, but the sellers, who were getting the higher prices, were not making unusually high profits. Indeed, they were generally making unusually low profits. Producers were not trying hard to produce more to sell at the higher prices. They were having great difficulty in selling their current output. Shopkeepers, instetad of being able to choose among eager buyers, were trying hard to persuade customers to come in and buy more. They were not limiting their sales of a scarce item to those who agreed to buy some profitable item. On the contrary, the customer was often given something with the item he bought or was given the right to buy something at an especially low price. Sellers were more polite than ever and more eager to sell than usual. They tried to make the stores more attractive and to help the customers find what they wanted, and to pack the purchases neatly and attractively.

In all sorts of ways they showed that this inflation was different from the usual kind of inflation. In the usual inflation the sellers find it easy to sell and buyers find it hard to buy (even if they have the money to pay for the goods). In this inflation it was the other way around. Buyers (if they had the money to pay the price) found it very easy to buy and sellers found it very difficult to sell. There was a *deficiency* of demand.

As a result of this perverse relationship, policy was paralyzed. The normal cure for inflation is to reduce the excess demand that is supposed to cause the inflation, but the existence of severe unemployment told us that we ought rather to do the opposite —we should increase total spending so as to mitigate the depression. The moment this was brought up for consideration storms of protest arose from respectable quarters warning that this would only feed the inflation.

When steps were then taken to stave off the inflation, even if only a little bit, by holding down the level of spending, unemployment increased while prices kept on rising more or less as before. Holding down spending, instead of checking the inflation of *prices*, had the effect of deflating the *economy*. The longstanding association of inflation with prosperity had evaporated. But instead of being set free for effective independent action to prevent inflation even while combating depression, we found ourselves frozen between the two evils. Buridan's legendary ass was unable to choose between two equidistant bundles of hay and so starved to death. We found ourselves forced to choose between greater unemployment if we moved one way and greater inflation if we moved the other way—but, perhaps this was because we limited ourselves to increases and decreases in the rate of spending. Is there perhaps some third direction in which we should move to escape from this dilemma?

Chapter 2

PRICE CONTROL

W E have found that concentrating on the volume of total spending leads us to policies which feed inflation if we move one way, and fosters depression if we move the other way, and so we seek a third way which may deliver us from the dilemma. A very simple solution beckons us. Why not simply stop inflation by pro-·nibiting people from raising wages and prices? Why not *freeze* the price level? Could this have stopped the inflation without bringing on the reduction in spending which causes unemployment to increase?

In the previous chapter we touched on what happens when prices are not increased in the face of excess demand. There we were considering the case where this occurred because the sellers, for one reason or another, did not want to raise the price. We saw that this led to the emergence of various other symptoms of excess demand. But now we approach the problem from a slightly different angle—or rather, from two such slightly different angles. In the first place, we want to consider the *enforced* prohibition of price increases, in the face of excess demand. In the second place, we want to consider whether it makes a difference if the prohibition is applied to *all* prices. (Wages are also included, since they too are prices—the prices of the various kinds of labor, and, indeed, rather important prices.) We shall find that there is a difference, but not a very comforting one.

We will first consider the effect of prohibiting only a particular price increase. Much the same consideration will apply if we consider the freezing of a number of prices provided that in total they do not cover a large part of the whole economy. This examination of price controls and their aftermath, interesting in itself, will be found especially useful in later chapters.

Price control, the legal prohibition of price increases in the face of excess demand, has happened many times—so many times, in fact, that it is possible to chart a kind of natural history of the course of events during the lifetime of price control.

Price control is instituted when there is a scarcity of some item. It becomes clear that there is not enough available for all the buyers to be able to buy as much as they would like to, but it is decided to prevent the buyers or the sellers from raising the price. Sometimes the price has already risen, and the price control is put in force to prevent the price from rising still further, and in some cases to roll it back to what it had been before.

The first effect is usually the establishment of a black market, where those who are not able to obtain the item at the legal price get it by paying the higher, illegal, price. This is hard to prevent, since both the buyer and the seller benefit from the transaction and nobody else need know about it. The item may disappear altogether from the open or "white" market. If the black market becomes important and widely used, it begins to appear less black and becomes a "gray" market, and ultimately even a "free" market, as contrasted with the official market that is likely to become "unfree."

What this means is that not only the price is regulated, but also the quantity one can buy. This occurs when price control does not drive the supply entirely to the black market. The legitimate sellers then have to deal with a demand for more of the item than they have available. They may, of course, only pretend not to exceed the legal price but in fact raise the price by various subterfuges. They may reduce portions, knowing that the customer will not dare complain. They may insist on tie-in sales, where the higher price is disguised as payment for the tied-in goods (which are not controlled and are very profitable). But even the complete avoidance of such subterfuges still leaves unsolved the basic problem. There is not enough to go round.

Perfectly honest and scrupulously legalistic sellers are still faced with the problem of who should get what is available, and who should do with less or do without. The seller will be tempted to sell to his friends and not to strangers or to people he does not like. He will even be tempted to consider as his friends those who are better customers and buy more of the other items on which he makes good profits, and he may not even realize that this is very close to the subterfuge of tie-in sales. Even if this is done with no bad intentions, it can be disastrous to poor people who cannot be such good customers, to strangers, or any others to whom he decides not to sell.

The rich, the charming, and the regular customers get much of the scarce item, while the poor, the unattractive, and the strangers find that when they come to buy, there is none left. The favored ones are served from "under-the-counter," as this has come to be called in countries plagued by such price controls. The price control, while intended to protect the poor from the high price that would restrict them to buying only very little of the item, has the effect of preventing them from getting any at all on the legal market; while on the black market, where they can buy as much as they can pay for, the price is much higher than the uncontrolled price would have been. This is because only a part of the scarce item gets to the black market; because those who are able to buy cheap on the legal market at the controlled price buy more than they would have bought in the absence of the price control; because the black market is less efficient than a legal market; and because the black marketeer has to be compensated for the additional hazards and costs of operating illegally.

If the seller is not only strictly honest and legal but even has a conscience that recognizes a social responsibility for the power that has been thrust upon him, there is still very little he can do. He will try to be fair in allocating scarce goods among different customers, limiting the amount he sells to any one of them so as to be able to sell some to all customers. But he is not in a position to do this at all effectively. He cannot tell if a customer asks for his allotment many times, or buys from many sellers, or resells for a higher price on the black market. Dissatisfaction with this kind of amateur rationing results in the development of official rationing systems under government auspices. This can be much fairer since it can more or less assure that everyone has only one ration book which entitles him to buy specified amounts of the various rationed items. It is clearly a great improvement over haphazard rationing by shopkeepers of different degrees of competence, as well as of different degrees of goodwill.

But discontent still continues to grow. The rationing authority, no matter how great a bureaucracy it builds up, cannot take into account the different needs of different individuals or families. It must treat different people as if they were identical, so the vegetarian has his ration of meat when he would rather have more fruit or vegetables, while the carnivorous customer gets the same ration of meat, which to him looks much too small, and has little use for his ration of the natural or organic foods that the vegetarian covets. Similar wasteful inefficiencies multiply as more and more goods are rationed; and more and more goods come to be rationed as the money saved from being able to buy the rationed goods at lower, controlled, prices becomes available for buying other goods. This increase in the demand for these other goods tends to cause their prices to be raised and then to be controlled. At the controlled prices their demand comes to exceed the supply, and these other commodities come to be added to the list of rationed goods.

The next stage in the natural history of price controls is the invention of devices for making rationing more flexible. Rationing is done by groups of commodities, and *ration points* are provided that have alternative uses. The same points can be used for steak as well as for hamburger (of course, for more hamburger than steak) and then not only for meat but also for fats and butter and milk and cheese. Similarly, instead of different ration points for shirts and socks, there are ration points for clothes, with a certain number of points for a pair of socks and another number of points for a shirt, etc., so that the available clothes can be distributed more in accordance with the different needs and tastes of different consumers.

But when this is done, some of the items will remain unsold. The consumers will be using the points for buying the more popular of the alternatives for which they are valid. These more popular items will be in such short supply that customers will not be able to get them even though they have the points required. They will be back again where they were before rationing was instituted, when they were not able to buy the goods even though they had the money to pay the (controlled) price. At this stage in the development of a more and more sophisticated rationing system, it is found necessary to keep on adjusting the number of points that are required for each of the items.

There are still higher stages of rationalization of a rationing system, but long before even this stage has been reached price control is usually abandoned—to the accompaniment of universal cheers.

It is clear that this description of the natural history of price control does not fit in with the present situation. Not only do we not have price control, but we do not even have the scarcities which give rise to it. It is useful for us to take this look at the nature of price control because proposals for dealing with our inflationary depression tend to be called price control and summarily dismissed. This sketch of what price control really looks like, helps us see to what extent such an identification is justified or not.

The price control we have considered covered only *some* of the prices, and most of the effects that we saw in its "natural history" resulted from this. Controlling some of the prices causes those who can get the items cheaply to use them wastefully. At the same time, it works undue hardship on those who have a greater need for them which they are prevented from satisfying. This is because price control makes the controlled price relatively low—relatively, that is, to uncontrolled prices—and causes buyers to switch to the cheaper price-controlled goods. The result is a still greater shortage of these goods, and those who do not succeed in getting them have to shift to less satisfactory—and more expensive—uncontrolled substitutes.

Such shifting to substitutes is not possible if price control is universal—if all prices and wages are controlled and we have what economists call *suppressed inflation* or *repressed inflation*. This is worse, not better. If only some items are subjected to price control, the possibility of spending the money left over on other items is a kind of safety valve. The uncontrolled items can become extremely expensive, and the excess spending can be drawn off from the economy through taxation of the item at purchase or through high taxation of the very large profits that may be made by those who sell them. Resentment at these very high profits is often responsible for the spread of price control to these other items even when they are goods that could be left only for the rich and not goods which must be made available for everybody. Such spreading of price control is one of the ways in which particular or selective price controls can become a general or even universal price control.

With universal price control the siphoning off of excess demand by expensive luxuries is prevented, and the pressure of the unspent money becomes greater. With nothing left for the money to buy, it is harder than ever to prevent the emergence of black markets, especially as they come to exist in almost all commodities. The most harmful effect is no longer the deprivation of the poor. At this stage in the development of price control the more important items will have been organized in relatively efficient rationing schemes that provide for a more reasonable distribution of what are considered necessities. The black market will consist of luxuries, of items which are not considered worth rationing because no great suffering is imposed on poor people unable to afford them.

The high black market prices for some of these luxuries arouse great resentment. This is because they look just like necessities. They consist of *additional quantities* of the necessities that are being rationed, and this is especially disturbing to those who are complaining about the meagerness of their rations. But there is really nothing worse about a rich man being able to buy more of something that is made available in limited quantities to everybody at a low price than it is for him to be able to buy something that looks quite different and which the poor man is used to doing without. It is too expensive and not so necessary—just like additional quantities of necessities. More harmful to society than the actual enjoyment of these black market luxuries by the rich, whether they look like natural luxuries or like more of some rationed "necessity," is the resentments that are generated. These are felt more strongly when they are seen not merely as the difference between being rich and being poor, but as the use of the illegal black market for frustrating the rationing system.

Much more serious than either of these resentments is the resulting disrespect for the law when wholesale violations come to be accepted as normal. The development of an attitude of toleration for the breaking of some laws easily spreads to tolerance of the breaking of other laws. Attempts to bolster respect by invoking legal penalties against the transgressors becomes impossible for the courts of law. Their time is taken up with these cases and they find that they are not able to deal with much more serious crimes. It becomes more and more difficult to get juries to convict offenders who are brought to court and for judges to sentence them, if it is known that hundreds of thousands or even millions of others are unapprehended though equally guilty. The habit of offenses being disregarded by the authorities—which is bound to develop in such circumstances—spreads to other offenses more or less related to the tolerated ones. More serious crimes also become more and more difficult to punish. They too tend either to be dealt with more and more leniently or to become practically unpunishable altogether.

Still worse things follow. On the one hand the failure of the courts to operate results in an increase of crime as more and more people discover that crime does pay. On the other hand when conscientious officers of the law find that the criminals they arrest with great difficulty and danger have ways of getting around the law, or consider the punishments they get as reasonable costs of operation that do little to hamper their activities, there is a strong temptation for them to take the law into their own hands. Some of these officers take it upon themselves to punish the criminals whom the courts cannot or will not or in any case do not punish. This, of course, is not only "police brutality" but shows contempt for the law by those whose duty it is to uphold the law. It leads to a much higher order of disrespect and disregard of the law in vicious circles.

These are some of the results that are at least encouraged by consistent attempts at universal price control, even if that is not the only source of such developments in our society. And unfortunately I do not think I am exaggerating. But my main purpose here is to point out that all this is strictly irrelevant for the subject of this book.

I find it useful to remind the reader of these dangers, not only because that is a social service, in any context, but because some regulations suggested later in this book are frequently denounced as price control. I want to make it clear that I am perhaps as well aware of the evils of price control as anybody. I am not soft on price control. What I will claim is that the proposals in this book do not involve price control and therefore do not bring about the evils that are justly associated with price control. Price control, we must remember, grows out of attempts to prevent the price from rising when there is not enough of an item to satisfy the demand at the existing price, when it is hard to buy but easy to sell, when it is not possible to increase the production of the item, or in the case of general price control when it is impossible to produce any more of things in general. It grows out of the usual kind of inflation in which there are shortages of everything. It is the absence of these symptoms, described in Chapter 1, that makes our inflation different and price control irrelevant. Our inflation is different from other inflations just because it does not have the conditions which give rise to price control. We are not suffering from shortages, either particular or general.

Any regulations that might be called for, and some will be suggested in later chapters, are *not* such as would create shortages where the economy would not be able to provide all that buyers would like to buy at the going price. Consequently they would not have the effect of leading to black markets and so on. Therefore, they are not price controls and would not lead to the evil results we have been considering.

My purpose here is to warn the readers against a natural tendency to identify *regulation* with price control because of some superficial similarities. This, however, is only a secondary purpose of the chapter. The primary purpose is to show, with much emphasis, that there is no salvation from any kind of inflation in any kind of price control.

Chapter 3

HOW DID WE
GET INTO THIS MESS?

I. Analysis

THE frustrations of our inflationary depression with its dilemmas, and the difficulties of escaping from them, grow out of faulty diagnosis—or rather out of a series of faulty diagnoses of what is wrong.

The first of these is the "classical" diagnosis of inflation as due to excessive total spending in the economy. According to this analysis, all the buyers in the economy taken together, households, businesses, governments, Federal, State and local, and foreigners buying the country's exports, are spending too much money. Too much means more than enough to buy, at the current prices, all the goods and services that the country is able to produce.

If the total quantity of the goods and services that the economy of the United States is able to produce is such that at the current prices it would sell for $1.0 trillion, but all the buyers together are spending $1.2 trillion, there will not be enough goods to go around. The buyers will, in effect, be trying to buy 120 per cent of what is available and naturally they cannot succeed. Some of the would-be buyers will have to do without, or with less than they wanted to buy. The natural result is an increase in prices. If prices rise by 20 per cent (on the average), $1.2 trillion will no longer be excessive. It will be just enough to buy all the goods available. What would have sold for $1.0 trillion at the previous prices now sells for $1.2 trillion.

We have seen in the previous chapter what happens if prices are not permitted to rise. A price control that attempts to stop the price rise when there is excess demand results in black markets, rationing, the development of a substitute and inferior system of pricing in "ration points" instead of in money, and finally the scrapping of controls. Price increases come to be accepted as the lesser evil. Higher prices are the natural result of excess spending. The way to prevent higher prices due to excess spending is to prevent the excess spending.

Inflation is often blamed on too much government spending, on government deficits, or on the creation of too much money, but these are not really different theories. Each of these turns out to be nothing but different ways in which total spending is increased and made excessive. If there is already enough spending and the government increases its spending (without, by taxing or borrowing, causing others to reduce their spending by an equivalent amount), this makes total spending too great. If the government reduces taxes without reducing its spending, this means running a deficit if the government was previously balancing its budget. Additional spending by the public out of its tax savings can make total spending too great. An increase in the quantity of money takes place through the easing of credit. This induces businesses to increase their spending in making use of the additional money borrowed. This too increases total spending and can make it excessive. All of these items are already covered by the increase in total spending that makes it excessive and so brings on the rising general price level which is inflation.

This fits in perfectly with the classical economic explanation of the formation of the particular price of a particular good in a free market. If buyers try to buy more of any item than is available, the excess of demand over supply will cause the price to rise. The price will rise until it has sufficiently reduced the quantity of the item that the buyers want to buy and increased the quantity that the sellers want to sell, so as to bring demand and supply into balance with each other. At this price every seller can sell as much as he wants to sell and every buyer is able to buy as much as he wants to buy. The price paid and the quantity bought will then stay where they are as long as there is no change in the conditions determining the eagerness of the buyers to buy or the interest of the sellers in selling.

Exactly the same happens in reverse when the buyers want to buy less than the sellers want to sell. The price will fall. This induces buyers to want to buy more and makes sellers less eager to sell, until the quantity the sellers want to sell and the quantity the buyers want to buy become equal. This will be the level at which the price paid and the quantity bought will settle down. The sellers are able to sell all that they want to sell and the buyers are able to buy all that they want to buy. We have the "equilibrium" price that equates demand and supply.

This is a very important part of economic theory, even though economists know that such a description of how individual prices are determined applies without modification only to highly competitive markets. The fault in the diagnosis consists of applying this theory, without the necessary modifications, to the determination of *the general price level*. The general price level is an average of *all* the prices in the economy. The most important of these are *not* determined by the forces of supply and demand in perfectly competitive markets as just described. The application of this competitive supply analysis to explain the determination of the general price level leads to what has been called the "classical" conclusion that there is no need for the government to concern itself with the question of whether total spending in the economy is too much or too little.

The argument is that if, with current prices, total spending should be more than sufficient to buy all the goods that the economy is able to supply, then the general price level will rise until the level of total spending is no longer excessive but just enough to buy all the goods at the higher prices. Conversely, if total spending should be insufficient to buy all the goods that the economy is able to supply, the general price level will fall until the level of spending is no longer insufficient to buy all the goods.

There is therefore no need for the authorities to worry about even the possibility of unemployment. Unemployment occurs if total spending is not sufficient to buy all the goods that would be produced in the economy if everybody who wanted to work was able to find employment. But if any insufficiency in total spending had the effect of reducing the price level, it would "self-destruct"! The level of total spending would no longer be insufficient! This would automatically cure the unemployment.

There remains the possibility of inflation and deflation of prices and wages. The total potential output of goods and services increases as improved techniques and additions to equipment increase the output per worker, and as the number of workers increases. If total spending on the purchase of the output of the economy increases at a greater rate than total output, prices in general will rise. There will be inflation. If total spending increases at a lesser rate, or if it decreases, there will be deflation.

The output per worker (productivity) and the number of

workers (the labor force) have been increasing at about 3% and 1% a year respectively so that total output could increase at 4% a year.

If the total of spending on the output of the economy increased at the same 4% rate, the general price level would be stationary. Every year 4% more money would be spent in buying the 4% more goods and services produced. If total spending increased at more than 4% a year, prices would rise. We would have inflation. Conversely, if total spending increased at less than 4% a year, or if it decreased, there would be a deflation of prices.

Because of the 3% increase in output per worker, wage rates would increase *relative to prices* by 3% a year. So would salaries as well as profit and interest incomes. If total spending just kept up with output (at our 4%) the price level would be stable. Wages would rise at 3% on the average, but cost per unit would remain the same because the 3% increase in wages (and in other expenses that go together with wage costs) would be offset by the 3% increase in output per wage earner. If cost and price remain the same, the difference between the two, which is the gross profit per unit of output would also remain the same. But *total* gross profit would increase at 4% because of the 4% increase in the total number of units produced— 3% more per worker with 1% more workers. *Total* wages would also increase at 4% a year for the same reason.

If total spending increased at 10% a year, prices would have to rise in the proportion of 104 to 110 or about 6%. Wage rates and other incomes would rise by the same 6% on top of the 3% due to increased productivity, altogether about 9%. Total wages and total incomes would rise about 10%.

This would make no difference to *real* wages and profits. The greater increase in prices would just about eat up the greater increase in money incomes. At 6% higher prices a 9% higher wage would buy just what a 3% higher wage would have bought at last year's prices. The same goes for the 9% increase in salary, profit, rent and interest incomes.

If total spending increased less than output this too would leave *real* wages and other real incomes unchanged. The lower money wages and other money incomes would be able to buy just as much because prices would be correspondingly lower. Thus if total spending increased by only 1%, prices would have to fall 3% to equate supply and demand. This fall in price would enable the previous total spending to buy 3% more of the 4% increase in output, and the remaining 1% of extra output would be purchased with the 1% extra spending (this would be the spending by the 1% increase in the number of workers and other income receivers).

The wage rate would not change at all. This absence of change is a 3% increase in the wage rate *relative* to prices which will have fallen 3%. The workers as well as all the others will get the same increase in real purchasing power as in all the other examples. But this time it will all take the form of their being able to buy 3% more with each dollar. The remaining 1% of extra output will be bought out of the extra 1% greater total money income earned by the 1% greater population.

Such inflations or deflations of prices would not affect the *total* real income of society, and would not matter at all if all incomes and prices rose or fell together, maintaining exactly the same proportions. But this could not work so exactly in the imperfect world in which we live, and this must be taken into account even with the simplified illustrations we have been using. Not all prices and all incomes will move to exactly the same degree. Those whose income rose relative to the price of the things they bought by more than the average 3% would gain from the unevennesses and imperfections in the price and income changes. Those whose income rose less than this average would stand to lose (relatively or absolutely). It would therefore be best, after all, for total spending to move in the same proportion as the increase in real output. The price level would then stay constant and the gains from the increase in productivity would most clearly be seen in the increase in money incomes.

If complete stability of the price level is not realizable, it is still better that the rate of growth of total spending should not depart very much from the rate of increase of productivity plus the rate of increase in the labor force. There would still be increases and decreases in individual real incomes for innumerable reasons quite unconnected with inflation or deflation of the general price level. But there would not be any additional disturbances due to inflation or deflation.

If total spending increased steadily at, say, 6% instead of the 4% that would give stability of the price level, we would have a fairly steady rate of price increase of 2% a year while wages and other incomes increased 5%. It would not be difficult to adjust to this, with everybody recognizing that the rate of increase in real incomes was still only 3%. There are even those who believe that a moderate rate of inflation, such as this, would make the economy work more smoothly, but this belief departs from the pure "classical" diagnosis of the nature of our inflation. We shall have to leave consideration of this till later. The essence of the classical analysis is that it sees inflation and deflation as the natural results of total spending increasing at a greater or smaller rate than the growth of total output.

Chapter 4

HOW DID WE
GET INTO THIS MESS?

II. *"Sound Finance"*

INFLATION and deflation would not be serious if we could depend on some natural forces that tend to keep total spending fairly stable. There would then be nothing much to worry about. There do exist such stabilizing factors. The classical approach is therefore to concentrate on the safeguarding of these stabilizing factors.

The basic stabilizing factor in the classical analysis is the quantity of money. If the quantity of money is stable there are limits to the degree to which total spending can vary. And if there is a tendency for the total quantity of money to increase slightly, total spending can increase too, just as is required to enable the gradually increasing total output to be bought at a fairly stable price level. Or alternatively, if the total quantity of money is stable but the invention of money substitutes enables total spending to be increased relative to the quantity of money, although only at a gradual rate, then complete stability in the quantity of money is compatible with the gradual increase in total spending required for a relatively stable price level.

Historically, the use of gold as money has provided a fairly stable quantity. It increased only gradually because the annual production of gold was small compared to the total stock of gold accumulated since time immemorial. The production of paper money was held in check by the convention that it had to be backed by gold. The invention of paper money could not increase the quantity of money as long as the paper money had to be fully backed by gold reserves. It was "golden paper."

The development of fractional reserves, whereby paper money was only partly backed by gold reserves, did increase the quantity of money, and this made possible a corresponding increase in total spending. But over the long run this was not very great in relation to the increase in population and productivity, so that the increase in total spending could remain within hailing distance of the increase in output. The development of banking led to further economies in the use of gold coin money and of gold-backed paper money, so that the same quantity of gold and paper money was compatible with much more total spending in the form of payment by check. And there have been other, less important, substitutes for earlier forms of money, such as traveller's checks and credit cards. But these developments too have been gradual and were accompanied by continuing growth of population and output per capita.

Consequently there was a kind of natural stability of the price level, upset only from time to time by the action of interfering governments. Great price inflations occurred when governments greatly increased the quantity of money. Occasionally price deflations occurred, though much more rarely and only to a much tinier degree, when these were reductions in the quantity of money.

The great inflations took place when governments practiced deficit finance on a large scale, paying their bills with newly created money instead of raising the money they needed by taking some of the existing money away from people by taxing them or borrowing from them. Such newly created money is possible only if governments break away from the principle of limiting money in accordance with its gold backing. Then paper money is no longer "golden paper." (Some forms of government borrowing are really the creation of new money, namely when the receipts given by government can be used like money and then in reality they *are* money.)

The classical analysis therefore leads to a basic policy rule for preventing inflation: government must refrain from *deficit financing* or from creating *fiat money*—paper money backed not by gold but only by the declaration of a "fiat" of the government. If governments balanced their budgets, spending only the money they took from the citizens in taxes, there could be no unnatural increase in the quantity of money and so no unnatural increase in spending out of relation to the output of goods and services in the economy.

The same rules, applied in reverse, would also protect us from deflation. The government should not engage in *surplus* financing or *destroy* money. It should not raise *more* in taxes than it spends. But this was less important since there is not at all the same temptation for governments to engage in surplus financing and money destruction as there is for governments to run deficits and create money. The latter enables them to spend money without having either to raise taxes or get into debt.

The combination of the two injunctions to the government: not to engage in deficit financing and not to engage in surplus financing, yields the single policy principle of balancing the government budget.

This way of looking at the causes of inflation and deflation, and the simple policy principles that follow from it, was so successfully taught by the economists of the last few hundred years that it earned the title of "Sound Finance." Its general acceptance however seems to be due less to the efforts of the economists to spread an understanding of the analysis sketched above than to the marvelous way in which "Sound Finance" coincided with well established principles for private individuals, families and businesses to keep solvent. The puritanical principle of not living beyond one's means was projected onto government by analogy. The raising of taxes by a government was identified with the earning of money by a worker or a business, so that spending by government in excess of its tax revenues was identified with an individual's spending more than he was earning, getting into debt and courting ruin. It became a commonplace to declare that deficit financing by the government would lead to bankruptcy!

The inapplicability of this concept to government resulted in an inevitable vagueness as to whether it would be the government or the country that was conceived of as being hauled into bankruptcy court and ordered by the magistrate not to borrow any more money without disclosing the bankruptcy, on pain of being sent to prison for fraud.

This, of course, was not what was intended by the economists who developed the analysis of inflation and deflation as caused only by too much total spending and too little total spending.

The purest form of the "Sound Finance" policy, which grows out of the classical analysis, is "laissez faire." It calls for the government to "leave things be"—to keep its hands off the creation or destruction of money and at the same time avoid borrowing and lending. The government should spend only the money that it takes away from citizens in taxes and thus never deliberately increase or decrease the level of spending but leave these to the natural forces of gold (and silver) production and the development of money substitutes. (This is the idea behind the widespread belief or feeling that the Central Bank—in the United States, the Federal Reserve System—should in some sense be independent of the government, or at least of the Treasury.)

A somewhat less pure but much more reasonable policy also grows out of the same classical analysis. This is the "neo-classical" analysis which combines classical analysis with a recognition that natural forces might not always increase the quantity of money to the degree required by the growth in total output (after allowing for the development of money substitutes.) This policy requires the government to control the creation of money and have it increase regularly by something like 3 or 4 per cent a year.

With the quantity of money thus protected from any vast fluctuations brought about by irresponsible governments, there could be only moderate changes in the price level. Total spending would still sometimes increase more than the volume of output and sometimes less. In the former case moderate increases in the price level would set things right, and in the latter case moderate declines in the price level would serve this purpose. Such minor inflations and deflations of the price level would keep the *real* volume of spending in line with the potential output. There would never be any very serious disturbance to the prosperity of the economy. In *real* terms there would always be the right amount of spending for full employment prosperity and progress, with real output limited only by the growth of productivity and the increase in the labor force.

In spite of fanatical support by businessmen who saw in it the practical wisdom that worked so well in their private affairs, the laissez faire policy collapsed with the recognition that inadequate total spending, instead of bringing about a deflation of prices and wages, brought about *depression* of the economy.

Prices and wages did not fall. Inadequate spending remained inadequate. The great depression of the 1930's brought this out as never before.

The basic point had been sensed by many monetary cranks but did not attain respectability until formulated by Lord Keynes in a way that fitted into the ways of thinking of the established economics profession. The basic proposition of the Keynesian "New Economics" was that "sound finance" must be replaced by government responsibility for preventing depression. Government must see to it that total spending is adequate to buy up, at current prices, the whole of potential output.

Even then, with many economists of the highest reputation supporting the Keynesian "New Economics," it was not possible to get the government to take more than some quite inadequate steps toward bringing total spending up to the level required for full employment. It was only the great increase in total spending brought about by World War II that demonstrated, for all to see, that an adequate increase in total spending could put to work the vast reserves of unused labor and other productive resources that had been idled in the great depression of the 1930's. Thus did the classical analysis come to be superseded by the Keynesian analysis and "sound finance" gave way to "The New Economics."

The essential contribution of the Keynesian analysis was the recognition that inadequate spending resulted in depression instead of in deflation. This recognition made possible the adoption of a policy that was responsible for the unprecedently long period of prosperity from 1961 to 1969. But we shall see in the next chapter how, by failing to deal with inflation, it lost its credentials as a remedy for depression, and was displaced by other policies which are responsible for our present inflationary depression.

Chapter 5

HOW DID WE
GET INTO THIS MESS?

III. Functional Finance

THE Keynesian displacement of sound finance rests essentially on its denial that there is an automatic cure for unemployment through deflation. Its point is that insufficient demand does not lead to the lowering of prices and wages which would make the smaller demand sufficient. This is because there is a rigidity downwards. Wages and prices are "sticky downward." They refuse to fall.

The discussion which clarified this matter can be condensed in the form of an imaginary and oversimplified debate between a crude Keynesian and a simple business man brought up on sound finance. The businessman points out that he knows from his own experience, confirmed by the experience of all his business friends, that if wages could be reduced even a little, he would be able to sell more of his product and employ more people. But the pigheadedness or stupidity or crookedness of the leaders of labor damages everybody, including the workers. They refuse to accept the slightly lower wage which would cure unemployment. If they would only accept a small wage cut his costs would go down and he would be able to expand his business and the employment it provides.

The Keynesian points out that while this is true for any single business it is not true for the economy as a whole. The increase in employment provided by the single business comes from undercutting his competitors' prices. Although he gets to employ more workers he does it by taking customers away from others who have to employ fewer workers. He has diminished unemployment in his factory, but not unemployment in the country as a whole. And that is what economists must be concerned about.

What we have here is a case of the fallacy of composition. What is true of any one of the firms taken by itself is not true of all of them taken together. The increase in the firm's employment is not an increase in total employment. It is a *substitution* of employment in one place where the employer can see it, for employment in another place in which he is not interested, but the economist has to be.

A second stage of the argument is reached when the businessman agrees that his first argument was unsatisfactory and promises not to try to palm off a substitution for an increase in employment again. He says: "Let us consider the economy as a whole. Suppose wages are reduced everywhere so that there is no question of workers shifting from one place to another. It would still be true that the wage cut would lower costs and thereby prices. At the lower prices more goods could be bought with the same income. If more goods are bought more will be produced, and more workers will be employed in making them. If prices keep on falling as long as there is insufficient spending, more and more goods will be bought with the same income, and more and more people will be employed, until prosperity is restored."

This second argument is also not acceptable to the Keynesian economist. He now points out a different error. What we have now is not the fallacy of composition but the impropriety of assuming that the income is the same. The reduction in wages is a reduction in the income of the workers. There is no reason for expecting a change in the degree of monopoly—the ratio of prices to costs. The prices of the products may therefore be expected to fall in the same proportion as costs, so that profits, the difference between cost and prices, would also fall in the same proportion. And if wages and profits fall in the same proportion total income too falls in the same proportion as prices, so that it would not be able to buy any more than before. Indeed if it were not for the lower prices the lower income would buy *less* than before and provide *less* employment.

It is true that if employment should increase then total income would not fall as much as prices. It might even increase. The income then would be able to buy more goods than before, and provide more employment. But this only shows that if you begin by assuming that employment has increased you can come out with the conclusion that employment has increased. We are still where we were at the beginning. There is here no vindication of the sound finance argument of an automatic cure of unemployment through falling prices.

The businessman then falls back on a third argument. He begins by agreeing that if wages were reduced, costs, prices, profits and total income could all very well fall in the same proportion as wages. He then goes on to argue that there still would be one thing which did not have to fall: namely, the quantity of money in the economy. At lower wages and prices with the same volume of employment, and therefore with a correspondingly lower level of money income too, the amount of money that people need to keep in their possession is also lower. The quantity of money in existence, which is also of course the quantity of money in the possession of everybody, has

39

however stayed the same. In general, therefore, people will find themselves in possession of more money than they need to hold.

They will then try to do something more useful with this unneeded or spare money. Basically, they will lend it out to earn interest, or use it to pay off debt so as to save interest payments. They may buy securities with it but that is only another way of lending. On the other side of the market, borrowers will not borrow so much because the money they already have has increased in real purchasing power and satisfies more of their needs. The increased readiness of lenders to lend and the decreased urgency of borrowers to borrow have the effect of lowering the terms on which lending takes place. The rate of interest falls. At the lower rate of interest additional investments become worthwhile and more investment expenditure takes place. This increases income. The increased income makes people spend more on consumption. Indeed a very large part of the increased income will be spent by those who receive it. This increases income again, with further increases in income and consumption, until income has increased by several times the increase in investment, and unemployment is correspondingly less. If there is still some unemployment a further reduction in wages will lead to further reductions in costs, prices, profits and money incomes, in the quantity of money people need to hold, and still lower interest rates. This will lead to further increases in investment and more increases in income and so on for further reductions in unemployment. Thus we have a mechanism set in motion which will automatically bring about full employment.

This last argument, number three, is logically unassailable. However, it has no practical applicability because the degree of price and wage flexibility required for it is unattainable. The small reduction in wages which would enable a business to undercut its competitors is not enough. What is needed is a sufficient reduction in wages and prices to bring about a sufficient increase in the real value of the existing money stock, to bring about in turn a sufficient increase in investment to bring the economy to full employment. That degree of wage flexibility does not exist, nor is there any practical possibility of bringing it about.

Furthermore, any attempts to bring about the required fall in prices by putting pressure on wage flexibility is likely to do more harm than good. This may seem strange but it follows from the nature of the resistance of wages and prices to deflation.

If all wages could suddenly be reduced by a large amount and all prices suddenly lowered correspondingly, then sound finance argument number 3 would stand. But first we would have to remove the power of the trade unions to prevent wages from falling in spite of unemployment. For that it would be necessary to overcome the much wider general sentiment, not only of workers but of the public in general, against wage reduction— the general feeling that it is only right and proper that in a modern and progressive society wages should rather always be rising.

The power of the trade unions and of workers generally to resist wage cuts can be overcome only by severe and continuing unemployment. Severe and continuing unemployment could be successful in this only to the degree that it succeeded in using up the reserves of the trade union for strike pay, and in using up the reserves and the credit of the unemployed workers. They would then be forced by starvation to overcome their antipathy to being "scabs." Such "success" could come only after considerable delay and severe unemployment and at first only in some sectors of the economy. A little later some other sectors

41

of the economy might be forced to give in. In this way there would be established an expectation of a gradually *declining* price level.

But what we need for our cure is not a declining but a *lower* price level. At a lower price level people don't need to hold so much money. They can lend some of it out and start the employment-increasing mechanism. A *declining* price level, however, works quite the wrong way. As soon as consumers see it and start expecting prices to go on falling for some time, they will postpone every possible purchase, waiting for prices to fall further. This would mean a decrease in spending and a worsening rather than an improvement in the condition of employment.

Investors will be even more discouraged from the additional spending that would have reduced unemployment. In the first place falling prices mean increasing value, or purchasing power, of money stocks. Holders of money will therefore be less eager to reduce their stocks of money by lending some of it out, so that there will not be as great a reduction as might be expected in the rate of interest. There might even be an increase. In the second place investors will also be induced to wait for the cose of investing to fall. And in the third place the decrease in consumer spending will leave unused productive capacity rather than a demand for investment in production. Here then, even more than in the production of consumption goods, *declining* prices and the *expectation* of declining prices are bad for employment. This is what we had in the 1930's. Prices did indeed fall, but that established an expectation of further price reductions and made things much worse before they could get any better.

The theoretical automatic cure of unemployment through price and wage flexibility is not practical. The degree of flexibility which could possibly be introduced is insufficient and only makes things worse. Even that will therefore not be applied by any government which wants to be re-elected and possibly not even by governments which do not depend on re-election but which for other reasons do not want to see a severe depression.

The failure of all three sound finance arguments leads to the adoption of a policy which grows out of the Keynesian approach—the policy of *functional finance*.

Functional finance is the policy which follows from a recognition of the responsibility of the government for keeping the total amount of spending in the whole economy *neither too great*, which would cause inflation, *nor too little*, which would cause depression. There are a number of different ways in which the government can do that.

One way is by changing the total amount of spending in the economy by spending more or spending less itself. It can buy more or buy less of whatever it is the government spends money on. It can bring about an equivalent result by operating on the other side of a market, by selling less or selling more of anything it has to sell.

Another way is to take less money away from people (by taxation) to enable them to spend more; or to take more away from them in heavier taxation so they will spend less. This too has a negative side consisting of the government's giving money to people instead of taking it away, as it has been doing more and more in various transfer payments. Giving more would cause people to spend more; giving less would cause them to spend less.

Yet another instrument in the hands of the government (including the Central Bank which in the last resort must be responsible to the government), is the borrowing and lending of money. Treasury or Central Bank borrowing from the public has the effect of decreasing the quantity of money in the hands of the public. This is likely to bring about a reduction in spending by the public. Treasury or Central Bank lending money, or repaying old borrowings, has the opposite effect. It increases the amount of money in the hands of the public and induces them to spend more.

There has been much debate on the relative effectiveness of the different instruments between those who stress fiscal policy (government spending and taxing) and those who stress monetary policy (the creation or destruction of money, or government borrowing and lending). But this noisy debate is not really relevant. For our present purpose it does not matter which instruments are used to bring about the changes in total spending required to carry out the functional finance policy of preventing both too much and too little total spending.

The basic difficulty encountered here derives from an unwarranted inversion of the tenets of functional finance. Functional finance says that if there is too much spending there will be inflation and if there is too little spending there will be depression. The illegitimate inversion (which may easily pass unnoticed) is to say that if there is not too much spending there will be no inflation and if there is not too little spending there will be no depression. This would mean that if we succeed in getting the right amount of spending all will be well. We will have neither inflation nor deflation nor depression. Perhaps "flation" would be the word.

Functional finance came to be applied with quite remarkable success. It is responsible for the longest period of prosperity in the history of the United States, from 1961 to 1969. But then new troubles began. We found ourselves suffering from inflation and depression at the same time. The authorities had discovered that they could check inflationary price movements by applying functional finance measures to decrease total spending. But then they observed that there was unemployment. This meant that there was too little spending. They took functional finance measures to increase the volume of spending and, sure enough, unemployment diminished. But then there were outcries against further inflation. Thus there arose a movement backward and forward, "Stop and Go" as it was called in England, between increasing total spending to reduce the depression and decreasing total spending to reduce the inflation. Flation—in the sense of avoiding both inflation and *depression*—could not be achieved by merely bringing about some "right amount" of total spending.

Functional finance seemed to be saying contradictory things. It seemed to be saying that there is too much spending—that is why there is inflation; and at the same time also declaring that there is too little spending—that is why there is depression. If we have inflation and depression at the same time, we have too much spending and too little spending at the same time.

This contradiction led to the loss of credibility of the Keynesian theory and of functional finance. It was discredited by seeming to conflict with observable reality in the same way as the classical theory had. The classical theory got into trouble because it spoke only of inflation and deflation. It left no room for depression and had to be rejected when the existence of depression was observed. Functional finance does not deal with the existence of inflation and depression at the same time. The observation of the coexistence of inflation and depression meant that we had to find a new theory to deal with this phenomenon, while a misinterpretation of functional finance led to the supposition that functional finance had to be rejected

45

as self-contradictory—that with the coexistence of inflation and depression it required us to believe that spending was both too much and too little at the same time.

This was not the case because functional finance does *not* deny that inflation can also come about for reasons other than too much spending. But while it leaves room for this it does not provide the other reasons, and so a new theory is needed even if functional finance is not rejected. The need for such a new theory led to the emergence of the idea of a different kind of inflation which I want to call Inflation II, to distinguish it from Inflation I. Inflation I is inflation caused by too much spending. Inflation II is caused in another way which we will discuss in Chapter 6.

Chapter 6

INFLATION II—
ADMINISTERED INFLATION

FUNCTIONAL finance differs from "sound finance" only on the deflation-depression issue. There is no difference between the two with respect to inflation. Both explain inflation as being caused by too much spending. The difference is only as to the effects of too little spending. "Sound Finance" holds that too little spending would cause deflation. Prices would fall until everything was put right. Functional finance holds that wages and prices would not fall, that we would be stuck with depression, and that the way out was not through deflation of prices but through deliberate adjustment of the volume of spending. Since the price level would not adjust itself to the volume of spending, it was necessary to adjust the volume of spending to the price level to provide sufficient spending at existing prices, and no depression.

The failure of functional finance to deal with our present state of coexisting inflation and depression is related to the way in which it dealt with the depression problem. The Keynesians stressed that wages and prices did not go down when there was insufficient demand, as they would be required to do according to the market price determination theory we have at various points called supply and demand, classical theory, and "sound finance." On this theory insufficient spending, which is the same thing as a deficiency of demand in relation to supply or an excess of supply in relation to demand, should make the price (or wage) fall. An excess of supply in relation to demand means that *the market is saying that prices should fall.*

But prices do not fall. The Keynesian explanation of this was that prices were sticky downwards. But this is no explanation at all. For what does sticky downwards mean? It means that when the market tells prices to go down, they don't. So that to say that prices do not go down because prices are sticky downwards is like saying that prices do not go down because they do not go down. My mother did this much more economically. When she did not know the answer to a question she simply said: "Because."

But there is a genuine explanation why wages and prices do not go down when there is a depression. They do not go down because they are being determined not by the supply and demand of the market but by *price and wage administrators* who are stronger than the market.

Take the case of wages. There is unemployment, which means an excess of supply over demand. Nevertheless wages do not go down because there are people who tell them not to.

These are representatives of the workers, through their trade unions, and of the employers. Sometimes there are also representatives of government and other interested groups. These people consider the matter. If in their bargaining they decide against a particular wage going down they say "don't go down," even when the market is saying "go down." And the wage listens to them and not to the market. It does not go down. Other people—price administrators—determine what particular prices should do. There may be insufficient demand in the sense that much more could and would be produced if more could be sold at the current price. Nevertheless the price will not fall because the price administrators say "no."

It may seem surprising that Keynes, the Keynesians and the "functional financiers" should have been satisfied with so flimsy a pretended explanation of why wages and prices do not fall in the face of deficient demand. I think the explanation of this is to be found in the extreme discomfort they would have felt, as well-trained economists and theorists, in explicitly dethroning determination by the market. That is the very center of the whole structure of economic theory and they were not ready for so great a revolution. So they swept it under the rug with the shame-faced "explanation" that prices were "sticky downwards." They might have thought that the sociologist, the psychologist, or the political scientist ought to be called in. "Let George do it!" Or that it is not really important why wages and prices do not go down. The important fact of course is to realize that they do not in fact go down and that we consequently have depression instead of deflation if we wait for them to go down. To avoid depression we have to adjust spending by functional finance. There is then no deficiency of demand and the market does not tell prices to go down. The question thus becomes academic and can be left for ever under the rug.

While it does not matter for dealing with the depression problem whether we have a proper explanation of why wages and prices do not go down, it turns out to be indispensable for explaining the co-existence of inflation with depression. Once we recognize that wages and prices do not fall because there are administrators who can effectively say "no" when the market is saying that they should fall, it would immediately occur to us that perhaps the vocabulary of the wage and price administrators might be expanded. Instead of merely being able to say "no" when the market is telling wages and prices to fall, in an excess of supply or a sufficiency of demand, the administrators might be able to say to prices "go up" when the market is telling them to stay where they are or maybe even go down.

This is the solution to our riddle. If inflation could be caused only by too much spending, then it could not co-exist with depression caused by too little spending. But if inflation is caused not by too much spending, but by administrators who raise wages and prices even when there is not enough spending, then there is no contradiction and the riddle is solved. Perhaps one should rather say the Gordian knot is cut, since the solution is not in accordance with the established rules of the game of theoretical economics.

This then is Inflation II, or administered inflation. It is the rising of wages and prices not because of excess demand, not because *buyers* are trying to buy more than it is possible to buy, but because of something which is being done by the sellers. And there is a symmetrical relationship between what the sellers are trying to do in Inflation II, and what the buyers try to do in Inflation I.

In Inflation I, or overspending inflation, the buyers try to buy more than one hundred per cent of what is available. Naturally, they can never succeed in doing that and they follow the adage: "If you fail, try, try, again." And so inflation can continue as long as the buyers can manage to keep on increasing the total amount of spending in their attempts to buy more than there is to buy.

The parallel behavior by the sellers in Inflation II consists of the producers trying to get, as their respective shares of the product in return for their work, payments that amount to more than 100% of the total product. To take the simplest possible model, we may suppose there are simply the workers and the capitalist employers. The workers insist on getting enough in wages to be able to buy 75% of the product. The capitalist employers insist on getting 35% of the product as their share. The workers succeed in obtaining wages which seem high enough to reach their objective. This they do through wage rates established by the wage administrators. But the price administrators, who set the prices of the products, represent the capitalist owners of the businesses. They set the prices at such a level that after paying the established wages, there will still be enough left for the capitalists to be able to buy their 35% of the product. If both of these succeeded, between them they would be able to buy 110% of the product and naturally they cannot succeed. What happens is that when the new prices are set the workers discover that their pay is not enough to buy their 75% and so they demand and obtain a further wage increase. This increase in wages now means that at the prevailing prices the capitalists are unable to get their 35%, and so they raise the prices again. Once more we have a continuing process of price inflation through the suppliers trying to get more than 100% of the product, naturally failing to do so, and trying again and again by raising wages and prices.

They would not be able to do so for long if the government (including the Central Bank) did not make use of the instruments of functional finance to increase the total volume of spending. If the volume of spending is not increased, every time the prices are raised the quantity of goods that can be sold will be diminished in the same proportion. If the prices go up 10%, that is in the proportion 10 to 11, and there is no change in total spending, the quantity of goods that can be sold will fall in the same proportion, i.e., in the proportion 11 to 10. If the attempts of the sellers to get more than 100% of the product continues and prices rise as much as 20%, i.e., in the proportion 10 to 12, the quantity of goods that can be sold will fall in that proportion, i.e., in the proportion 12 to 10.

Thus it might seem that Inflation II is just like Inflation I in that it depends upon total spending being increased by the monetary and fiscal policy of the government. But there is a very important difference. In the case of Inflation I, if the government takes steps to slow down the increase in total spending all that happens is that the inflation slows down. If slowed to a sufficient degree, it stops being excessive altogether and we have no inflation at all. This would be the case if total spending were increasing at the same rate as total output was increasing (as a result of the increasing productivity of a grow-ing number of workers). But we would still have prosperity un-less the government overdid it and we moved from too much spending to too little spending—i.e., if it caused total spending to be less than enough to buy the total product of full em-ployment. If the government did not overdo it, it could stop inflation by holding down total spending without doing any harm to the economy.

This is not the case for Inflation II. If the authorities resolutely prevent any increase in total spending, sales will go down in proportion to the increase in prices. Employment will fall correspondingly since people will not continue to be employed in producing things which are not being sold.

It is in order to prevent such depression, which can be quite catastrophic, that government takes measures to increase the total volume of spending. It does this either by increasing the quantity of money, or by increasing the volume of spending in other ways—e.g., by buying more itself, or reducing taxes so that others will spend more, or by a combination of all the instruments which it has for increasing the volume of total spending.

We can now see the basic anatomy of Inflation II. It is a tri-partite administered inflation. There are the administrators of the wages who raise wages, and their usual explanation is that they have to do so because prices are rising. Then there are the administrators of the prices of the products. They raise the prices, and their explanation is that they have to do so because costs are being raised by the increasing wages. And finally there is the third set of administrators—the total spending administrators. These consist of the fiscal agents of the government and the controllers of the quantity of money. They take steps to increase total spending in order to prevent the depression which otherwise would overwhelm the economy. Each set of administrators can quite honestly believe that it is only the fault of the others that it has to participate in the inflationary process of Inflation II.

This kind of inflation has been given a series of different names. It has been called *wage push inflation,* in contrast to demand pull, to stress that it is the increase in wages which is responsible for the increase in costs and thereby in prices, rather than the insistence of buyers trying to buy more than there is. This was felt by some to put too much of the onus on labor. It has been called *mark-up inflation,* referring to the degree to which the capitalists or business, the sellers of the products, raised prices above costs in trying to increase their share of the product. This too was considered too one-sided. The term *sellers' inflation* was invented to include both workers and employers, the sellers of labor power as well as the sellers of products, as responsible for inflation. Perhaps more enlightening is the name *administered inflation*. It is the failure of the market to operate—the prevention of the market from operating by the administrators, which provides the basic explanation of the failure of the classical theory, and which was insufficiently indicated by the Keynesian reference to wages and prices being sticky downwards. Administered inflation seems to be for the time being the most satisfying name for this phenomenon.

Once the phenomenon is understood, it should not be too difficult to figure out the appropriate steps for dealing with the situation. It is clear that inflation is undesirable, whether it is Inflation I or Inflation II, and it would be good to prevent it or to cure the economy of it. But before we go into that we have to consider a further development of administered inflation in the following chapter, which deals with Inflationary Depression.

Chapter 7

INFLATIONARY DEPRESSION—
A CASE OF MISTAKEN IDENTITY

INFLATION I is a condition of rising prices due to attempts by buyers to buy more than is available. It can continue at a constant rate or at an increasing rate, or at a diminishing rate, depending upon what happens to the volume of total spending. Inflation II is an administered inflation resulting from the interaction of three sets of administrators: wage administrators, price administrators, and spending administrators. It too can continue at a constant, an increasing, or a decreasing rate. This depends on the rate at which wage and price administrators raise wages and prices in their attempts to obtain shares that add up to more than 100% of what is being produced.

Inflation I, being due to too much spending, can not co-exist with depression or even recession or indeed any level of economic activity less than full employment. This is because inadequate employment can arise only if there is some inadequacy of total spending; and there cannot be too much spending and too little spending at the same time. There is no such incompatibility in the case of Inflation II. There would however be no reason for expecting Inflation II to be accompanied by any depression if the spending administrators brought about sufficient total spending to enable the total output of full employment to be bought at the prices determined by the wage and price administrators.

If the spending administrators did this, it would be extremely difficult to distinguish between Inflation I and Inflation II. But if total spending is not sufficient to permit the total output of full employment to be bought, and the inflation is accompanied by depression or recession, it is easy to see that we have not Inflation I but Inflation II. After all, there cannot be too much spending if it is clearly shown by the depression or recession that there is too little spending.

The question then is why do the spending administrators not provide sufficient total spending so that we can enjoy the benefits of full employment? The basic reason for this is an unreadiness to accept the idea of Inflation II. The spending administrators cannot completely free themselves from the traditional belief that inflation is always of the Inflation I type —that it is always caused by, and must be due to, too much spending. They are rather uncomfortable and feel somewhat guilty about their part in the inflationary process, and they increase total spending only reluctantly and inadequately, so that it is not enough to maintain prosperity. That is why we have depression with inflation. At the same time there is great pressure on the government to stop inflation by holding down total spending. This, of course, is exactly the right remedy for Inflation I, but it is not the remedy for Inflation II.

When I say it is not the remedy for Inflation II, I should perhaps hedge a little. It is theoretically possible for Inflation II to be slowed down and even stopped by simply not providing the additional spending. But such a policy would never be applied because the degree of depression required is much more severe than any government would be willing to impose. It would call for a high level of unemployment for a very long time (see Chapter 5) to eliminate the "stickiness downward" of wages and prices. As in that connection it would call for a catastrophic depression traumatic enough to destroy the power of wage and price administration and to break down the public attitudes and group pressures that support the price and wage administrators.

But although the anti-spending prejudice is never carried anywhere near what would be needed to stop Inflation II, the authorities do take various measures to hold down total spending so that it is not enough to buy all that could be made under full employment. And we do have a recession serious enough to reduce the GNP by some 6 or 7 per cent—some 70 billion dollars a year. We would think this would make it clear enough that we are not suffering from too much demand. Nevertheless, we are continually being faced by claims that there must indeed be too much demand, charges that the economy is "overheated," declarations that inflation must be stopped "at all costs," and ascriptions of inflation to increases in the quantity of money.

By trying to stop inflation by holding down total spending, but not holding it down too much, because we do not want to allow too much depression, we manage to get the worst of both worlds. We get an "inflationary depression." It has also been called "depressionary inflation," "recessionary inflation," and has even given rise to the awful word "stagflation" combined of stagnation and inflation.

I first saw this kind of situation in operation a number of years ago in Israel, and I found the parable of the stinking fish very effective in showing how one can get the worst of both worlds. The story tells of a victim of the local autocrat

57

in a Russian township. He is sentenced to choose among three punishments: to eat a dish of stinking fish, to receive a hundred lashes, or to be fined a thousand rubles. The victim chooses to eat the stinking fish, but after having eaten most of it he finds it quite impossible to continue and so agrees to submit to the lashes. After receiving the greater part of the lashes, he feels that he is near death and so he pays the thousand rubles, which he could have done in the first place. I am not sure that the parable would be as effective in the United States as in Israel. In any case it is a very faulty parable insofar as it suggests that the evils of deflation and of inflation are of comparable magnitude; but if we can get away from the dogma according to which inflation is an infinite evil (so that it must be stopped "at all costs") and look at the actual damage done by the two evils, we find that depression is many, many times more damaging than inflation.

Consider the harm done by one per cent of additional inflation and compare it with the harm done by an additional one per cent of unemployment. An additional 1% of unemployment occurs only in response to a much larger decrease in sales and in output. When a firm's output decreases, not all kinds of employees are fired. More salesmen might even be hired in an attempt to bolster sales. Those involved in fixed costs, janitors, bookkeepers and many others, are kept on. Some employees are kept on, even though there is not much for them to do, because of a fear that it would be difficult to replace them later. The result is that 1% of additional unemployment indicates a 3% loss in output. In the United States, where the gross national product is over a trillion dollars, 1% of additional unemployment shows a loss of 3% of GNP, which comes to more than 30 billion dollars a year.

An additional 1% of inflation does mean that buyers lose

1% of what they are buying for each dollar they spend, and there is a strong temptation to count this as if it were a measure of the social loss from inflation. We saw, in Chapter 1, how President Nixon (before he "became a Keynesian") fell into this trap. Inflation is sometimes called a tax and occasionally even "the worst kind of tax." Indeed, it is not adjusted to the ability to pay, or chosen because it is considered better than other taxes on some other grounds.

However all this is a mistake. Inflation does not constitute a reduction in the goods available for people to buy. The idea that the buyer's loss from inflation can be treated as a social loss contravenes the first principle of elementary economics: the principle of remembering that if anybody pays any money somebody else must be getting it. Every 1% increase in prices, although it means that the buyers have to pay 1% more, also means that the sellers receive 1% more. Since both the sellers and the buyers are members of the society, society in the aggregate neither loses nor gains. Indeed most people are both buyers and sellers, at different times of the week or even of the day; so that the greater part of the losses when buying and the gains when selling cancel out, and perhaps only one quarter of the 1% of the national income involved is an actual transfer from some people to other people. This net transfer of ¼ of 1% from the buyers to the sellers changes the distribution of income and wealth, but there is no more reason for supposing that the new distribution is worse than the old distribution than for supposing that it is better. Most of the changes would be neutral. Some might be considered improvements in that they are shifts from people whom we consider less deserving to people whom we consider more deserving, and some the converse; so that the improvements and the deteriorations could be considered to offset each other.

There will however be a fraction, certainly not more than ¼ of the transfer, which we would strongly object to. This is the transfer from poor people with relatively fixed incomes who are impoverished by the inflation and whom we would like to have protected. The loss by these unfortunates amounts to ¼ of ¼ of the 1%, or 1/16 of 1% of the national income. The loss should be corrected and can be corrected by collecting money from others—if possible from those who have gained from the inflation, but otherwise from the population at large—in order to compensate the particularly unfortunate victims of inflation. This again is a transfer, not a loss.

There is a real loss involved in the actual operations—in the employment of people engaged in collecting and distributing these monies, and in checking whether there has not been some cheating by those who should be paying the taxes, or by those who are claiming the benefits. If we allow say 25% of the total amount of the transfer as expenses of the operation it would amount to a loss of ¼ of the 1/16 of the 1%, or 1/64 of 1% of the GNP. According to this very rough calculation, the 3% of GNP loss from 1% more unemployment is 192 times as great. It will suffice to say that depression is something like a hundred times as bad as inflation.

We would be remiss to leave the matter here. By far the worst result of choosing depression is not so much the loss of 30 billion dollars for each additional percentage of unemployed, compared to the much smaller loss that would be incurred in correcting the serious injustices of an additional 1% of inflation. Much more important than the absolute loss in income is the damage to the people on whom unemployment is concentrated; for indeed it is only the concentration of unemployment which makes it a real evil. If the unemployment were evenly spread over the whole population the additional 1% of unemployment would only mean about half a week's work off each year. And the 30 billion dollars would merely be the value of this part of the annual vacation. But high percentages of unemployment and long periods of unemployment are being concentrated on the members of minorities of race, color, creed, age and lack of skill. That is what is making many in these groups feel that they have no place in society, alienating them, turning them into enemies of our order—into problems which threaten the stability of the whole society. And all this is the result of the *limited* application of the cure that permits us to speak of recession rather than depression.

In short, the attempt to cure inflation by holding down the volume of spending amounts to applying a remedy with side effects enormously more harmful than the disease.

A resolute attempt to stop inflation with this remedy at all costs would mean establishing a depression severe enough, and lasting long enough, to destroy the organizations of society which give the wage and price administrators their power over wages and prices. In such a process the patient would expire before the disease was arrested. Fortunately the side effects are so visible that there is no likelihood at all of this remedy's being applied in the doses required for a full "cure." Like the stinking fish and the lashes in the story it will be rejected before it goes too far. Indeed the New Economic Policy of August 15, 1971, is nothing but society's self-protective turning away from exclusive reliance on this cure.

The persistence of this treatment of Inflation II—administered inflation—by the appropriate cure for Inflation I—overspending inflation—can be explained, in part, by a couple of misunderstandings and distractions. One of the most important is an identification of the increase in total spending (due to the spending administrators' not daring to hold down total spending too much) with *excess demand.* Indeed we often find figures which show that total spending has increased, being paraded as proof that demand is excessive. We have seen that if wages and prices are being pushed up by wage and price administrators, total spending, even if it is increasing, will be too little, and there will be depression as long as it is not increased sufficiently to enable full employment output to be sold at the increasing prices. However I have found that it is not at all easy to teach my students not to confuse an *increasing* volume of total spending with an *excessive* volume of total spending, and to remember that only the latter causes Inflation I.

Another reason for the persistent, if moderated, application of the wrong medicine is a debate which has distracted attention from the real issue. This is the debate as to whether the volume of spending depends more on monetary policy or on fiscal policy. It is sometimes taken to be a debate for or against Keynesianism with Keynes in the role of fiscalist. But Keynes is just as much a monetarist as a fiscalist. Indeed in his book, *The General Theory of Employment, Interest, and Money,* which started the Keynesian Revolution and on which functional finance is based, money plays a central role. The supply of money determines the rate of interest, which controls the volume of investment. This in turn influences income, and through income, consumption, and thus works back again on income to determine the volume of total spending and consequently the level of employment.

The fiscalists, who are strangely called "the Keynesians," are those who emphasize the importance of people's income on total spending. They point out that an increase in investment or in government spending will increase income. People spend more on consumption when their income is greater, and this increases other people's income, and *their* consumption, and still other incomes, and so on. The effect of the original increase on total income is *multiplied*. This is called the *multiplier* and is identified with Keynesianism because this is a part of Keynes's book which fits easily into economics text books. The monetarists stress the relation of the quantity of money to total spending. If people discover that their stock of money is more than they think necessary, they may spend some of it. More probably they will lend some of it. This will cheapen the terms on which money is loaned, inducing more spending by the borrowers. This is a debate in which there can be no doubt that both sides are right—except in their condemnation of each other. In this both are wrong.

Sometimes the debate turns into the essentially different, but nevertheless related issue, as to which of these two forces would be stronger in isolation. On this the monetarists would win. There is no limit to the degree to which the quantity of money can be increased, and thereby total spending and total income increased, while there are definite limits to the degree to which total spending can be increased if the quantity of money is not increased. But since there is never any necessity for depending on only one of these instruments the debate seems to me to be an extraordinary waste of time. What is much more serious is that the debate distracts attention from the necessity of treating Inflation II differently from Inflation I. Since Inflation II is not caused by too much spending, it is completely beside the point whether the imagined excess demand should be blamed on too generous a policy of creating money or on too generous a fiscal policy of stimulating invest-ment or consumption and activating the "multiplier."

The essential point is really a very simple one: we suffer

from inflationary depression because of the attempt to cure Inflation II, which is not due to excessive spending, by applying the wrong medicine—the medicine which is exactly appropriate to Inflation I, namely the removal of some of the spending. If spending is not excessive, and inflation is caused by something else, then the removal of some of the spending inevitably has the effect of making total spending insufficient and so we have the depression at the same time as the inflation. Unfortunately it seems impossible to ward off the doctors who administer this wrong medicine as long as we are suffering from some kind of inflation. We will therefore continue to suffer from this until we discover a way of dealing with Inflation II. The most important reason for finding an appropriate treatment for Inflation II is that it will save us from the wrong medicine.

Chapter 8

INCOMES POLICY

W E have seen how treating *Inflation II*—administered inflation—with the remedy that is appropriate for *Inflation I*—overspending inflation
—is the wrong treatment and leads to very
bad results. It consists of treating *Inflation II* by reducing
the amount of total spending, as if its cause were too much
spending. The result is inflationary depression. The right treatment for Inflation II is to try to remove the cause, which is
not too much spending, but the raising of wages and prices by
wage and price administrators. This forces the spending administrators to provide additional spending on pain of allowing an
intolerable degree of depression to come about.

One way of dealing with Inflation II would be to get rid of
the administrators, so that the competitive market would
determine prices. We would then be prone only to contract
Inflation I, and that only if there is too much total spending.
We would be able to avoid that by applying functional finance.
Unfortunately, there does not seem to be any way of getting
rid of the administrators. The next best thing is to regulate the
administrators so that they will administer prices in a way

which will avoid inflation and thus also inflationary depression. Such regulation of wage and price administrators is called *Incomes Policy*.

The regulation of administrators would have to cause them to administer wages and prices in a way similar to what would have been achieved in a competitive market. The first objective is price *stability* or the avoidance of inflation. This would mean administering wages in such a way that, on the average, they would rise at the same rate at which productivity was increasing. Costs of production on the average would then remain constant, and therefore the average price or price level could remain constant while providing the same margin of profit or mark-up of price over cost. Since the increase in productivity is expected to continue to be about 3% a year, this would mean a continuous wage increase of 3% a year, perhaps even made automatic at 1% every 4 months.

It would not do to leave it at that, however, inasmuch as this would freeze the relationships among individual wages and not provide any of the *flexibility* which the economy needs in order to adjust to continuing changes in demand for different kinds of products, in the technology of producing different items, in the availability of resources for producing them, and other influences. Wages would all be rising, but if they rise in the same proportion, their relations are fixed. This would prevent the market mechanism from serving the purpose of indicating where workers should be encouraged to go, and where to leave.

To serve this purpose differential wage increases are needed, which will reflect the tightness or looseness of the particular labor market. In places where labor is particularly tight because there has been an increase in demand for the product or because workers have been drawn away for some other purpose, it is desirable to induce more workers to come from other areas where unemployment is higher than average. In low unemployment areas wages should therefore rise by more than 3%—say by 5% a year. The opposite should apply to areas where unemployment is very high—say more than twice the national average. Here wages should rise at only, say, 1% a year. These should be the rules to govern the wage administrators so as to bring about average price *stability* and relative wage and price *flexibility*.

The higher wages in tight labor areas would have a number of salutary effects. They would raise the cost, and therefore the prices, of these products relative to others. This would induce consumers to shift from buying these products to buying products made in areas where there is more unemployment. This would lead unemployment to even out. It would induce workers to move to areas where increased demand has led to low unemployment. And the converse would also be true. There would be encouragement of demand for the cheapened products in areas where a very high level of unemployment has reduced the rate of wage increase. There would be a third effect in bringing about a greater fairness of relative wages. Since wages would be rising relative to other wages in places where labor was tight, this is just what should happen. The tightness of a labor market means that the existing conditions of work and pay are not sufficiently attractive to induce workers to come in. Conversely, in areas where the percentage of unemployment is very high, wages would rise less. This too works for greater fairness insofar as the high percentage of unemployment is an indication that people are going there or are staying there because the total conditions of work and pay are sufficiently attractive to hold them, or to induce them to move into those areas, even though their chances of landing a job are not too good. The rules would even out the relative attractiveness of the different occupations in the different parts of the economy.

The regulation of price administration would consist of checking to see that undue advantage was not taken by businesses, particularly monopolistic businesses, to raise their prices relative to their costs. That is to say the profit per unit, the difference between the price and the cost of production, should not become exorbitant. There is indeed no reason why the power of monopolists to obtain exorbitant profits should be increased by the regulations here suggested any more than that it should be diminished. On the contrary, insofar as the incomes policy would result in some scrutiny, existing exorbitant profits could be exposed and corrected. However, we are concerned here with the treatment of inflation. Diminishing the degree of monopoly in the economy is a separate objective which deserves to be pursued quite independently of whether there is any inflation problem or not. For the purpose of an anti-inflationary incomes policy, by far the most important regulation concerns wage administrators. Although care must be taken to see that there is no discrimination against labor, one must not take it for granted that greater emphasis on the regulation of wage administrators than of price administrators is necessarily prejudicial to labor.

It will of course not be possible to carry out an incomes policy without its general acceptance by the public as necessary for the maintenance of price stability and high employment. If there is such general agreement, there will be voluntary, if sometimes grumbling, acquiescence in the wages and prices set by administrators.

One cannot depend entirely on that, but fortunately a couple of sanctions of last resort are available to fall back on if public opinion or lighter sanctions should fail, and these should be amply adequate even though they do not involve any blood-letting.

The next problem is to consider what sanctions would be needed to cause the regulations to be obeyed. It is important to see that no Draconian measures will be called for. It will not be necessary to put employers in jail for paying more than the present wage increases. (Earning exorbitant profits by monopolistic restriction is another thing.)

The first sanction is that no payment of wage increases over and above those indicated by the regulated administrators should be counted as a legitimate cost to be deducted by employers in figuring their taxable income. As long as employers are willing to pay higher wages out of their own pockets there need be no interference. They will not be able to pass it on in higher prices of their products by claiming the excess wages as legitimate costs.

This, however, would not be sufficient. They would still be able to raise the prices of the products so as to make large enough "profits" to be able to say that they are paying the higher wages out of the pockets into which they put these "profits." Such "profits" would of course be fictional. They are really costs paid out in wages over and above those permitted by the regulation. This subterfuge can be prevented by having special high taxes on exorbitant profit—any profit per unit of product considerably out of line—either in comparison with what it had been before the incomes policy, or on more general criteria. Employers would therefore be encouraged to avoid such excess "profits" (which could be taxed even more than 100%) by lowering their prices and either refraining from paying excessive wages or really paying them out of their own pockets.

When I first began to propose incomes policies of this kind, something like a quarter of a century ago, I encountered, with painful frequency, the declaration that an incomes policy would solve the problem of the unemployed by giving them all jobs in administering wages and prices. But this is hardly a serious criticism. It fails to notice that we already have wage and price administrators. All we need is some regulation of the administrators. In the words of Kenneth Galbraith, "It is easier to administer anything if it is already being administered." Of course some people will be employed in doing that, and at the present time we have just seen, in Phase Two of Nixon's "Economic Policy," something of the magnitudes required. It involves perhaps some thousands of civil servants. This is certainly quite negligible when we consider that successful application of this policy would put to work in their regular occupations not thousands or tens of thousands of workers but one or two millions of those who are now unemployed.

There will of course be innumerable objections to this policy, primarily because it has not yet been done. Perhaps the most powerful is the identification of this regulation with price control. We have seen in Chapter 2 that price control consists of an attempt to prevent the market from operating when there is excess demand, or in other words a shortage of supply. Price control tries to prevent the price from rising to clear the market. Clearly our whole problem is that this condition is exactly what is *not* found. There is no shortage of supply. There is instead a shortage of demand. There is too little, not too much, spending for full employment. The regulation of the administrators, rather than being an attempt to interfere with the market, is really an attempt to stop wage and price administrators from interfering with the market by making wages and prices rise when in many cases the market conditions of supply

70

and demand are telling them to fall. The regulations would instruct administrators to make wages and prices behave more as they would in a competitive market.

It would be too much to claim that these regulations would be equivalent to an active competitive market. The market is a much more sensitive instrument which can deal with millions of different degrees of adjustment of prices and wages. All that even a perfectly working incomes policy can do is to provide a very rough or primitive imitation of the market. But even this crude imitation would be an enormous improvement on an inflationary depression with 6% unemployment. We have seen that it is possible to manage with no more than 3½% unemployment. There is reason to believe that better development of institutions for spreading information about job opportunities, for retraining and for improving mobility would make possible considerably lower percentages of unemployment without inflation. This is because as crude a substitute for the competitive market as the incomes policy is, it restores the full efficacy of functional finance.

A special word of warning is necessary here to remind the reader that the rule that wages should rise at a rate equal to the increase in productivity strictly applies only to the *average* of all wages, and strictly refers only to the *average* increase in productivity in the economy as a whole. The deviations from the 3% and 5% rates of increase in some cases and the 1% increase in other cases, must be determined *only* by the degree of employment or unemployment in the different parts of the economy.

This repetition is necessary because there have been, and there will certainly continue to be, demands by workers in industries where there has been a more than average increase in productivity to claim that this entitles them to a more than average increase in wages—a "productivity" wage increase. The only force behind the argument is the interest of the particular workers in getting higher pay, no matter what reasons they may like to put forward.

An increase in productivity in a particular industry may indeed have the effect of changing conditions in a way which would call for the higher wage increase; but it may also do the opposite. It will call for the higher rate of wage increase (5% instead of 3%) if the increased productivity, by reducing the price of the product, causes such a great increase in the amount demanded that the number of workers needed in the industry increases, and the unemployment rate falls to less than half the national average. The higher rate of wage increase is then appropriate and serves to induce workers to come into this area from other parts of the economy.

But this need not be the case. It could very well be that the increase in productivity which lowers the price causes only a small increase in demand, and this larger amount could now be made by fewer men than were necessary before. The percentage of unemployment in this area could then rise to more than twice the national average! The increase in productivity should in this case lower the rate of wage increase to the 1% rate. What is required is that the workers released here should go to other parts of the economy where they are needed more.

In the next chapter we shall see that certain complications closely related to the way incomes policies were managed resulted in their breakdown in many countries in the recent past We shall consider where they went wrong.

Chapter 9

THE LATE
WAGE-PRICE GUIDEPOSTS

T HE incomes policy remedy for Inflation II—administered inflation—discussed rather sketchily in the last chapter, will no doubt be recognized as what the United States has called wage-price guideposts. These resemble various attempts made in other countries to deal with inflation from the supply rather than the demand side, by regulating increases in wages and prices. Wage-price guideposts are credited with having slowed down the rate of inflation to some extent, perhaps by as much as 1% a year in the United States. But in nearly all cases they have broken down and been more or less abandoned.

There are a number of reasons for this. One is their unpopularity because they are confused in the public mind with price control. This happens even though, as we have tried to show, they are almost the exact opposite of price control insofar as they endeavor to protect or replace the market mechanism instead of trying to prevent it from operating. There is one particularly interesting reason for their breaking down and that is their over-concentration on stability to the neglect of flexibility.

The first objective of an incomes policy is of course *stability* of the general price level, for which it is necessary to keep average wages from rising more than *average* productivity. The very name wage-price guideposts betrays a concentration on these averages. The averages come to be identified with the guideposts, conceived as guiding all prices to be stable and all wages to rise at the national average rate of increase in productivity. This would keep average costs stable, and that would permit prices to be stable. The need for flexibility—for greater and smaller wage increases at different points in the economy—although clearly envisaged by the authors of the guidelines, was ignored or forgotten by the general public.

This over-concentration on stability to the neglect of flexibility was seriously aggravated by a psychological error on the part of those in charge of the wage-price guideposts. In the United States the average rate of increase in productivity has been around 3% a year. It was figured out at 3.2% and this number was unfortunately given wide publicity and had far too great an impact. The .2% gave the impression of extreme exactness, or maybe that it was a very scientific number, and so it was given much more attention than it deserved. This led to the idea that 3.2% was in fact the rate at which every wage should be increased. It came to be felt that anybody who tried to get more than 3.2% was cheating or sabotaging the attempt to stop inflation, and that anybody who received less than 3.2% was being cheated.

It seems clear that this was not the intention of those who set up the scheme, but by using this exact-looking number, they did give that impression to non-economists who did not read the small print. And so the idea was established that 3.2% was the correct rate of wage increase—that everybody was entitled to 3.2% and nobody to more.

We have seen that using the same rate of increase for everybody freezes the ratios among wages. This leaves no way for the economy to adjust to changes in conditions of demand, supply, technology, imports, exports and so on. Where there is a relative excess of labor, and wages should rise by less than 3.2%, the rigid 3.2% rule would mean that workers in this area would remain unemployed even if the total amount of spending in the economy as a whole was adequate. But the worst trouble comes in the opposite condition, where there is relative scarcity of labor. In these areas wages should be required to rise by more than 3.2% but the regulated wage administrators were obeying the 3.2% rule.

In this case there is once more a conflict between what the market says and what the wage administrator says, but they have changed sides. Now the market is telling the wages to rise by more than 3.2%, say by 6% or 10%, and the regulated administrators are telling the wages they may not rise by more than 3.2%; and now the prices will listen to the market rather than to the administrators. They will disregard the administrators' attempts to keep the increase to 3.2%.

Here we really do have price control. The wage administrators by allowing this rule are not protecting the market, or substituting for it. They are preventing it from working. And price control has to break down as we have seen in Chapter 2.

This is exactly what happened. There were some areas in the economy where there was a shortage of labor, and wages had to rise by 10% or more to clear the market. This was the "instruction" given by the market—by "supply and demand." The controls then broke down. Workers in space engineering, certain military activities, and a few other such tight labor markets listened to the market, flouted the guideposts, and demanded wage increases of 10% or more; and employers, competing with each other, granted the increases.

This would not have been fatal but for the widespread consensus that a uniform rate of wage increase was proper for everybody. The principle of uniformity was apparently even more powerful than the magic number 3.2. When workers everywhere else saw that some were getting increases of 6, 8, or 10%, they said: "why not us too?" And they then began to disregard the wage-price guideposts and to demand larger wage increases, which they got. The guideposts collapsed. They broke down because of insufficient attention to the second task of incomes policy, the provision of flexibility. The wage-price guideposts attempt at an incomes policy died of rigidity of the relative wages.

Future attempts at an incomes policy will probably pay more attention to flexibility, but it will not be easy to prevent this history from repeating itself. Flexibility means that some wages will be raised by more than the average increase in productivity, and some by less. To many this will appear not as the impartial following of an objective rule as explained in the previous chapter, but as *exceptions*. Indeed, some of the departures from the average rate of increase will be exceptions—concessions to group pressures which cannot be resisted. The latter, instead of improving relative prices by bringing flexibility, may very well do exactly the opposite: raising those wages which are already relatively too high, while keeping down those which are relatively too low.

However, even if this danger were completely overcome and we had proper working flexibility in an incomes policy, there still is very little hope that Inflation II would be cured by this measure, even though it is directed at the operative forces which keep the Inflation II going. The reason for this is that Inflation

II, just like Inflation I, has built into it an impossible objective.

Inflation I has an impossible objective in the buyers' trying to buy more than there is available. Of course they can never succeed in doing that, and so inflation continues as long as excess spending continues. It stops when the reason for its existence, excessive demand, comes to an end. This takes place when prices reach a level at which the spending is no longer excessive. Unless there is a further increase in total spending, people will no longer be trying to buy more than is available. They were trying to buy more than is available simply because they had enough income or money to be able to do so, and there was no reason why each individual should not spend the money he had available.

Inflation II has a more durable basis. This is the intention of workers and employers, or more generally all the owners of the factors of production, to get, as payment for their participation in producing the national income, shares in it which add up to more than 100%. This unattainable objective is not as easy to remove as the unattainable objective of buyers trying to buy more than is available. Monetary and fiscal policies can control total spending so that it is not too great, and this is the function of functional finance. But functional finance cannot so easily persuade workers and employers to be satisfied with smaller percentages of the total product.

It is of course true that the rules of the incomes policy we have been suggesting, for limiting the rate of increase of wages and maintaining a steady markup of price over cost, would indeed stop inflation. But to do this it would be necessary to get the producers to accept shares that amount to not more than 100% of the total product. If the shares they consider themselves entitled to amount to more than 100% they will reject the suggested incomes policy as being unfair. The workers will see in the incomes policy an attempt to reduce their share of the product for the benefit of the employers, the employers will see in it an attempt to reduce their share for the benefit of the workers. Their insistence on "disallowed" higher wages and higher prices will destroy the incomes policy. It will break down because it cannot succeed in carrying out the miracle of giving the various contributors to output more than 100% of what they produce.

One solution, although it is debatable whether it deserves the name of solution, is an inflationary depression brought about by a refusal to permit total spending to increase in parallel with the "disollowed" increases in wages and prices. As the "disallowed" wages and prices keep rising the severity of the inflationary depression will increase until there is so much unemployment that the eagerness of people to obtain work or sell products is strong enough to overcome the idea of what is a fair wage, or a fair markup, and they will no longer demand shares that amount to more than 100% of the total product. Whether our social fabric could withstand the strains would then be the important issue.

Governments have not been ready to impose this degree of depression. They have instead tried to achieve a compromise of inflationary *recession* as if to prove that they were at least *trying* to buy off more severe inflation with this concession. But such a reduction in the rate of inflation does not stay bought. The inflation accelerates for a number of reasons including the failure of the incomes policy to provide flexibility. The most important reason is the failure of the parties to production to get the impossible sum of shares—more than 100% of the product. Even if all the other conditions are fully satisfied, this condition can never be satisfied. Inflation II turns out to be essentially insoluble except by the politically unacceptable extreme depression. The hope of avoiding inflationary depression or inflationary recession rests on the possibility that our inflation is not Inflation II but some other kind—perhaps an Inflation III—which, unlike Inflation II, is amenable to a satisfactory solution.

Chapter 10

INFLATION III—
EXPECTATIONAL INFLATION

I NFLATION I, which is caused by too much spending, can be cured by a functional finance policy of reducing total spending so that it is no longer too great. The cause of inflation is thus removed, and inflation is stopped. However, the current inflation is not Inflation I and this is not the cure. We have seen that Inflation II, or administered inflation, which is due to the producers trying to get among themselves more than 100% of the product, would be cured if we could regulate the wage and price administrators and prevent them from raising wages by more than the rate of increase in productivity, and by preventing prices from rising relative to costs. But we also saw that this would be very difficult if not impossible as long as the producers—the workers and the employers —were trying, between them, to get shares of the product that added up to more than 100% of it. They would not agree to the kind of regulation which would make this clearly impossible for any to attempt. It was always of course impossible for all to achieve. However, there is hope for dealing with the inflation, and the inflationary depression, if it should turn out that what we have is not Inflation II, but Inflation III.

Inflation III looks very much like Inflation II. It also is a tripartite administered inflation. It also involves wage administrators raising wages by more than productivity, price administrators raising prices, and spending administrators increasing the volume of spending. Also, as in Inflation II, if the spending administrators hold total spending below what is required for full employment at the administered wages and prices, they turn the administered inflation into an inflationary recession. The difference is that in Inflation III the wage and price increases are directed by the various bodies not at obtaining larger shares, but only at protecting themselves from getting smaller shares.

In Inflation III workers and capitalists would be quite satisfied to keep on getting the shares they are actually getting, plus the 3% per annum extra from the increasing productivity. This is not to deny that they would be even more pleased if they could in addition get the benefits from a higher level of employment, with additional wage income and profit income in which again all could participate. None of the objectives is inherently impossible to achieve.

Inflation III is essentially a defensive rather than an aggressive administered inflation, and it is based upon the expectation of inflation—normally the expectation of the continuation of an inflation which has been going on for some time. If future inflation is expected at a rate of 6% per annum (perhaps because that is what it was in the recent past), and is expected to continue at that rate, the workers will insist on a 6% increase in wages over and above the increase warranted by the increasing productivity. Prices will rise by 6% because costs will be rising by 6%. The wage increase would do no more than protect the share that the workers were already getting and the price increase would do no more than protect the share which the capitalists were already getting. What they all were already getting was of course not more than 100%, and therefore this objective is achievable. The spending administrators would of course have to keep on providing the extra spending needed to enable the level of activity and output to be maintained at the higher and rising prices.

It should be noted that nothing is said here as to how the inflation began. Clear thinking on this subject is frequently disturbed by the tendency to change the subject from what to do about the present condition into what started the inflation in tne first place, and what should have been done then to prevent it.

There is fairly general agreement that the present inflation was started by increased government expenditure at the time of the expansion of the Vietnam War. The war was too unpopular for the taxes to be imposed which would have offset the increase in government spending. This temporarily created too much total spending and a demand inflation—a little bit of Inflation I. This excess spending did not last very long. Increasing productivity very soon more than overtook the increased expenditure on the Vietnam War, but by then the expectation of continuing inflation had taken hold.

But this is history, and it is perfectly possible for an Inflation III—an expectational inflation—to be started in many other ways. Anything which causes prices to rise for a while can start it going. In this case the initiating price increase seems to have been caused by a bout of excessive demand, or Inflation I. It could have been caused by tax increases. It could have been started by an increase in the price of imports because of something which happened in foreign countries. It could have been started by an organizational change in the trade union movement, which permitted a sudden increase in wages and therefore in costs and prices. But for our present purpose it does not matter what was the historical cause. An expectation of future inflation, and attempts by workers and their employers to protect themselves from it, gives us Inflation III which on the surface is not distinguishable from Inflation II.

If what we have is indeed Inflation III, a defensive and not an aggressive administered inflation, then an incomes policy could work. The regulations which reduced the rate of increase in money incomes would equally reduce the rate of increase in prices, so that real incomes would initially be unaffected and would continue to increase on account of increasing productivity at the 3% or so at which this is going on.

We have been considering incomes policy as directed at achieving price stability. For this it would establish a rate of wage increase averaging 3%, with of course the greater and smaller increases in different parts of the economy in order to provide the necessary flexibility. Incomes policy may also be directed at a more modest objective. In Phase Two of President Nixon's New Economic Policy the objective was to limit the rate of inflation to $2\frac{1}{2}$% per annum. This would call for an average wage increase of $5\frac{1}{2}$% per annum.

Since stability of the price level is almost universally considered to be more desirable than a $2\frac{1}{2}$% per annum inflation of prices, the 3% rate of increase in wages would seem to be more desirable. The $5\frac{1}{2}$% target was adopted instead, however, on account of an apparent belief that stability is something that we should only try to attain very gradually. I have not been able to understand why this is necessary.

If this was only mock modesty—a polite way of saying that the resistances to wage increases of only 3% were too great and only a $5\frac{1}{2}$% average income ceiling could be hoped for, given the political pressures—then, of course, there is nothing more that the economist can say. We have to limit ourselves to the politically possible. The only thing that I would like to say is that I would prefer to have such an adjustment openly recognized as abdication in the face of pressure, giving in to a kind of blackmail, or threats of strikes or lockouts or what not, rather than to disguise it as virtuous gradualism.

The difference between the two targets is that if we could apply the 3% average wage rate increase with the corresponding zero price increase, the effect would be to remove the expectation of a 6% inflation and to replace it by an expectation of price stability; whereas the 5½% average wage increase would replace the expectation of 6% inflation with an expectation of a 2½% inflation. Presumably if we succeeded in the latter we might then consider the possibility of repeating the experiment and reestablishing a still lower rate of expectation, perhaps even the zero rate of expected inflation.

What is of interest is what whichever of these we do, whichever the rate at which inflation is stabilized, zero per cent, 1%, 1½%, or 2½%, or any other rate of inflation, we would still be able to avoid the terrible medicine of trying to cure inflation by creating depression. We would be able to restore full employment by providing the corresponding volume of enough spending. There would remain no reason for restricting the volume of spending below what is necessary to buy the total potential output of the economy in full employment.

Once the chosen rate of inflation is established the expectations of its continuance would become self-fulfilling. Functional finance could then maintain the stable (even if not zero) rate of inflation by not allowing total spending to become more than enough to buy the whole of the potential output at full employment at the chosen rate of increase of prices.

If we had chosen the 2½% rate of price inflation, which

goes with the 5½% average rate of wage increases, workers would find that their real wages are not only protected but rising at the 3% provided by increasing productivity. The receivers of profit would similarly be getting the 3% a year increase in their income from increasing productivity. On top of that everyone would be enjoying the much more important benefit of a high level of employment. The wage and price administrators would continue to grant the 5½% average wage increase, with its plusses and minuses, and prices on the average would continue to rise at 2½%, fulfilling everybody's expectations. There would be stability: not indeed stability of prices but stability in the rate of inflation, enabling functional finance to maintain full employment.

We must note now how something strange has happened here to the theory of supply and demand—what "the market" tells price to do. What is usually understood by supply and demand, by market determination of prices, is that if the supply is greater than the demand for anything the price will fall, and if the demand is greater than the supply the price will rise. If the demand and the supply are equal the price will not change. But we have just been describing a situation in which we had full employment, we had sufficient total spending to give us full employment at the rising prices, there was no excess demand and no insufficiency of demand. Nevertheless prices were rising at 2½% (or one of the other rates of increases chosen). How can this be?

The answer is that the traditional formulation requires amendment. There is *a hidden assumption* which needs to be spelled out. The hidden assumption is that there exists *an expectation of stable prices.*

On this assumption the normal or classical argument is exactly right. An excess of demand raises the prices, disturbs this expectation, and establishes an expectation of rising prices. Conversely, if we had flexibility downwards, a deficiency of demand would cause prices to fall and establish an expectation of falling prices. (Of course, we do not have flexibility downward, and so we would get not deflation of prices—and of price expectations—but depression instead.)

But if we start with an expectation other than that of stable prices we have to reformulate the classical proposition, spelling out the assumption about price expectations. We have to say that if demand is greater than supply, prices rise more than was expected. The previous expectation is shown to have been wrong and a new expectation of a *greater* increase in prices is established; and conversely, if demand is less than supply, the market forces would call for a reduction in the rate of expectation of rising prices (assuming we have downward flexibility of expectations).

Let me put this in figures: Suppose people were expecting a price increase of 6% per annum and an Inflation III was in progress with just sufficient demand for full employment. The equality of supply to demand would not bring about stable prices. It would merely confirm and strengthen the fulfilled expectation of prices rising at 6%. Everything had worked out as expected, and prices would continue to rise at 6% as long as the demand was kept level with supply at the increasing prices—as long as the increase in total spending was just sufficient (10%) to buy the increasing volume of goods (4%) produced by the increasing labor force (1%) with the increasing output per man (3%) at the rising prices (6%). If the demand were greater than that, there would be an increase in the rate of actual and expected price increases, say to 8%. If the demand were less than that, there would be a decrease in both to, say, 3%. All this assumes the market is in control. If we were in an Inflation III instead, an incomes policy could similarly affect the actual and expected rate of inflation.

Our conclusion then is that if in fact we are faced not with Inflation II, but with Inflation III, an incomes policy which provided for flexibility as well as for stability could succeed either in stopping the inflation, or in stabilizing it at some lower rate. The declared target of Phase Two was to stabilize the inflation at some 2½% per annum, with an average wage increase of 5½% per annum. There seems to be no basic economic reason why zero inflation could not have been chosen right at the beginning. It would have yielded all the benefits of any other rate of inflation in addition to the great convenience of a stable value of money.

There remain two basic difficulties. The first is that maybe we have Inflation II, rather than Inflation III. If that is the case incomes policy will not succeed because its regulations would become acceptable only if either (a) a degree of depression is brought about severe enough and lasting long enough to break the demand for impossible shares or (b) by some other means aggressive Inflation II is transformed into defensive Inflation III. The other difficulty is that even if we are in an Inflation III situation there will be resistance to the application of this policy, based on the same expectation of inflation. We turn to these difficulties in Chapter 11.

Chapter 11

DISINFLATION

W E have considered the argument that Inflation III, based on the expectation of inflation and only defensive, would make it possible for an incomes policy to work. The incomes policy would not be called upon to perform the miracle of giving the different partners in production more than 100% of what they produce. But there still would remain the problem of getting the program sufficiently acceptable by workers and employers to be carried out in practice. Here we come up against the difficulty that the very cause of Inflation III is the reason why it would be very difficult if possible at all to apply the cure of an incomes policy. If there is a firmly established expectation that prices are going to keep on rising at, say, 6% a year, a proposal to limit wages to an average increase of 3% a year would sound like a proposal for a 3% cut in wages. If prices will indeed rise at 6%, $103 next year will be able to buy no more than $97 today. Workers would naturally reject any such proposal and, on this understanding of it they would be perfectly justified. For there is indeed no reason why there should be any reduction in the real wage. On the contrary, increasing productivity is making it possible for real wages, the actual goods that workers can buy with their wages, to be increasing at 3% a year even while leaving a similar increase for all the other members of society.

The economist would indeed tell them that if there were an agreement to have a 3% a year average wage increase, and the rate of markup was kept from increasing, there would in fact be no increase in prices. The 3% increase in money wages would give them the same 3% real increase that a 9% increase would give them with a 6% price inflation. But economists have learned that there is not sufficient trust in economists for this to be believed. At the very best the workers would say: "Well, let us see prices stop rising first, and then we'll see if we'd be satisfied with a 3% increase in money wages." The price setters on the other hand would say: "Why, we are ready in fact to *reduce* our prices if wages don't increase at all. Even if wages increase, but at no more than 3%, the increase in productivity would permit us to keep prices stable. But let us see wages responding first." This is the impasse due to the insufficiency of faith in the economists' analysis—a fact which economists must take properly into account.

One way of getting the workers to understand that there is really no intention to reduce their real wages is to have a cost of living allowance to protect them from the effects of inflation. They could then agree to a 3% increase in the basic wage, together with a cost of living allowance which could give them another 6% as long as prices were rising at 6%. If it were accepted there would be no pressure for increasing the rate of pay by more than the average productivity of 3% plus the 6% cost of living allowance. Money wages would thus be rising at 9% and costs at 6%. In the absence of any change in the rate of markup the inflation would continue smoothly at a 6% rate of increase in prices and a 9% rate of increase in wages.

It might seem that very little had been accomplished. The inflation would not have been stopped. But the most important of the goals would indeed have been achieved. The inflation would have been *stabilized*. The escalation of the inflation would have been stopped, and it is the fear of escalation of inflation which gives force to the attempts to check inflation by engineering a depression. We could enjoy full employment.

We would of course have to consider what adjustments would be needed to make life more comfortable with a constant rate of inflation. That it is possible to make such adjustments is pretty clear from the history of countries where inflation has been going on for quite some time at much greater rates than ours. Various devices have been developed to protect those who would suffer most severely from inflation, so as to make it possible for life to continue. In Brazil for example inflation has been going on for a long time at rates between 20% and 90% a year and yet the economy has been progressing and a rate of growth of output of 9% a year is claimed. By comparison, the United States's economy has been growing at about 3½% and managed, in the last year, with the help of administered depression, to touch zero growth in real terms. The excitement in the United States over a 6% inflation seems quite comical to the Brazilians.

However, most of the devices for making life more livable under inflation consist essentially of developing inferior substitutes for a stable unit of money. It involves using other items instead of normal currency for various purposes. In some countries the cost of living index becomes practically a unit of account. In Brazil a similar function is played by the minimum wage which is charged every month or so to keep up with prices. The minimum wage has become a kind of unit of account. An over-parking fine, for example, is set at so many times the daily minimum wage. It is of course much less convenient than simply using the dollar and arranging for it to be a stable unit of account, but for this to work money wages would have to rise by no more than the 3% productivity increase.

The problem of insufficient trust or faith in the economist for workers to agree to a money wage rising at no more than productivity, can be met by a device which involves a much smaller amount of trust. It would consist of getting the workers to try a less complete cost of living allowance to see whether the economists were telling the truth in promising that this would get them the combined benefits of maintaining the 3% increase in real income, moving toward a stable price level, and winning a better chance of reaching and maintaining full employment.

We would say to the workers: "Agree to accept a cost of living allowance only very slightly smaller and you will see that as a matter of fact no real loss will be involved. There will be a correspondingly smaller increase in the price level." There could also be a guarantee of a restitution of the sacrifice if this should for some reason not work out.

The device can be illustrated with some very simple figures. Suppose it was agreed to accept a cost of living allowance one percentage point smaller than the rate of increase in prices in the previous period—say a year, though shorter periods would be better. Then if prices had been rising at 6% there would be a wage increase of not 9% but 8%, consisting of 3% for productivity plus 5% of cost of living allowance on account of the 6% increase in prices during the previous period. As a result of this, costs would rise not at 6% but at 5%, and the increase in prices would also be 5% with no change in the rate of markup. The next period, the cost of living allowance would be not 5% but 4% so that the total wage increase would be 4% plus 3% or 7%, and with the 3% increase in productivity there would be only a 4% increase in costs and in prices. The next period the inflation would be only 3%, then 2%, then 1% and finally 0% after 6 periods, each with one percentage point of disinflation.

A guarantee to assure the workers that they had nothing to lose by the experiment could take the form of undertaking to repay the 1% cut in the cost of living allowance if the expected 1% reduction in the inflation failed to materialize. Such a guarantee would have to be provided by the government. It would not do for the employers to give such a guarantee because they would have to put aside the 1% in case the plan failed and they were called upon to make the restitution. The employers would have to consider this potential obligation as a cost and would therefore not reduce their product price increase. The fear of failure would ensure the failure of the plan. The guarantee would therefore have to be an undertaking by the government so that it would not appear as a cost of production which would be reflected in price. There would of course be objections to the government's giving such a guarantee. It is a question of a little faith by the government instead of a little faith by the workers.

When I first outlined a scheme of this kind I received compliments on my ingenuity and expressions of doubt as to its realism. The device was considered "interesting but not practical." In the summer of 1970 I spent a couple of months in Brazil and discovered that the Brazilian authorities had been doing something very similar for a number of years. Their wage regulation gave over-generous wage increases on account of productivity, but they more than made up for this by giving much smaller allowance for the increase in the cost of living. The total wage increases permitted were less than the sum of the cost of living plus the increase in productivity, and the inflation was indeed disinflated. In the course of some five years the rate of inflation was reduced from somewhere between 80% and 90% to 20% a year. When I repeated in Brazil some of the lectures I had given on this topic in the U.S., their reaction was quite different. They couldn't see why my colleagues in the States had thought it was so ingenious. In the U.S. they had said "interesting but not practical." In Brazil they said "perfectly practical but not very interesting."

I think I must agree with my colleagues that the disinflation device is not very practical in the United States. The United States does not have a government as strong or trade unions as weak as Brazil's. The U.S. government cannot simply dictate disinflation. In Israel, although the trade unions are much stronger than in the U.S., there was a development similar to that in Brazil. Inflation was reduced from over 20% a year to less than 5%. (There has been some increase since, but the conditions are rather special.) But the United States does not have trade union leaders who put responsibility for the health of the country above demagogic advocacy of meaningless, because inflationary, increases in money wages. Indeed the reactions of the leaders of the trade union movement in the United States to President Nixon's antiinflation policy have shown even less responsibility than I had expected.

The purpose of the disinflation device is gradually to remove the expectation of inflation. The most effective way of removing this expectation is to roll down the actual inflation on which the expectation is based. This is the function of the gradual, step by step, reduction of the rate of increase in costs and in prices. It calls for a relatively small amount of faith—the willingness of workers to risk the one per cent gap in the cost of living allowance which they would get back in reduced inflation, and the willingness of the government to underwrite the risk of the device's not working. As always the weightier objective is to stop the inflationary depression induced by restriction of total demand, a reflex response conditioned by past experiences of Inflation I, but triggered by any inflation whether it is one for which the response is appropriate or not. Lacking any probable agreement to the disinflation device we ask ourselves whether there is not another way. We turn to another such way in the next chapter.

Chapter 12

THE FREEZE

"**I**F the patient won't give up his inflationary expectations gradually, we'll have to give him the shock treatment —a broad wage and price freeze." This is the prescription President Nixon announced on August 15th, 1971. The freeze is the first part of a two-phase alternative policy to the gradual disinflation described in Chapter 11.

This freeze had some similarities to the "repressed inflation" discussed in Chapter 2 on Price Control in that it applied not to some prices only, but to almost all prices and wages. Like repressed inflation or general price control it does not disturb the efficiency of the market mechanism by making some prices lower than others the way selective price controls do. But it is fundamentally different from repressed inflation in that it does not produce a general shortage of everything at the frozen prices. It is not an attempt to deal with too much spending— with excess demand—by forbidding prices in general to rise when the market is telling them to rise. The crisis that led to the freeze was just the reverse of this—a state of recession or depression with high unemployment because of a *deficiency* of demand—*too little* spending. It is because of this that it differs from repressed inflation—or any other kind of price control—in that there are no shortages, no shifting to less beneficial use of resources, no need for rationing and all the other phenomena arising from price controls. In short the purpose of the freeze is not to *suppress the symptoms* of Inflation I—rising prices due to excess demand—but to *remove the root cause* of Inflation III —the expectation of future inflation.

If wages and prices could stay frozen for a sufficiently long period, the memory of inflation might perhaps fade away, and the expectation of further inflation disappear. When this happened the freeze could be lifted, or allowed to thaw away. If total spending could then be prevented from becoming either excessive or deficient we could have price stability with full employment, and wages rising again with productivity. But such a simple breaking of inflationary expectations is almost impossible for two basic reasons.

The first reason is that the introduction of the freeze inevitably involves a series of *injustices*. In the preceding inflation some wages and prices will just have been raised before the freeze was imposed, while other wages and prices were expected to rise after the freeze was imposed. There clearly is an injustice between the two groups of people involved. Those who were prevented by the freeze from benefiting from wage or price increases would no doubt say that the time chosen was wrong.

This is inevitable because the increases in wages and prices are not smooth and uniform, but take place in jumps. Particular wage rates are changed with the expiration of a contract, or planned for a year or two years after the contract has been negotiated. The same is true of prices, as annual models of various products have their prices established or as a new annual or quarterly catalog is issued. Consequently, at the moment the freeze was established there were bound to be some lucky ones who had just recently had their wages or prices increased, and some unlucky ones whose wage or price increases were due in the very near future and were stopped by the freeze. The unlucky ones could complain, with considerable justice, that they had been treated unfairly. If the freeze had gone into effect *after* their wages or prices had been raised, they would then have been able to buy everything at the frozen prices while benefiting from the increased prices of what they themselves were selling. This injustice cannot be avoided no matter when the freeze is imposed. Any time chosen will seem the wrong time to some. There will always be some whose increases come just before the freeze and others who are caught with their prices down.

The second reason is perhaps even more important than the first. As time goes on the freeze brings about increasing *inefficiency* in the economy. The initial injustice of the freeze consists of different effects on different members of society, depending on the date on which prices and wages are frozen. But the inefficiency appears not at the beginning of the freeze, but only later on, and then it grows in importance as time progresses. At the beginning of the freeze prices are more or less appropriate to existing conditions, but as time goes on conditions change. Some things become more difficult to produce, perhaps because it is harder and harder to make more of an item in response to increased demand. But the appropriate price increase is prevented by the freeze. Another item would have become cheaper, either because an increase or a decrease in demand reduced the cost of producing it, or because changes in technology made it possible for the item to be produced with a smaller quantity of resources or out of different resources which cost less. But there will be a great reluctance to reduce a price which it might not be possible to raise again. The existing frozen prices thus become less and less appropriate as conditions change.

In the absence of the freeze the relative prices—the ratios of the prices to each other—would have changed. With no freeze and no inflation the price decreases would have balanced the increases, leaving the general level of prices, the average price, unchanged. With inflation going on, the general price level rises, but some prices would have risen more than others in response to changes in demand and in technology, and the change in *relative prices* required for the efficiency of the economy could still take place.

With prices frozen, the economy cannot respond as efficiently to the changes. The price increase which would have induced increased output of the goods for which the need had increased relatively to the difficulty of producing them, now does not come about. The price mechanism thus cannot perform its function of inducing ingenious and alert profit seekers to produce more of these goods instead of goods which have come to be needed less urgently or which have become harder to produce.

The growing inefficiency of the economy is due, not to the *level* of prices in general being lower, but to their *fixity* or *rigidity* relative to each other. This should not be surprising since rigidity, after all, is of the essence of freezing.

The rigidity of the economy under the freeze of wages and prices thus becomes an increasing burden. Coming on top of the initial injustices due to the differential impact of the freeze, which must hit some people at a worse time than others, it makes the freeze more and more difficult to maintain. More and more concessions may have to be made either in the interest of fairness or in response to political pressures and threats of strikes, lockouts and other troubles. Consequently, only a limited amount of time is made available by the freeze for developing a lasting solution to the inflation.

Increasing inefficiency will therefore add to the resentments, objections, complaints, demands for exceptions, and modifications that after some time would lead to the thawing of the freeze and its ultimate disappearance. The problem indeed is exactly the same as that discussed above when we considered the *relative* freezing of the wage-price guideposts which concentrated on stability without paying adequate attention to flexibility. The guideposts did not attempt to freeze wages absolutely, but the 3.2% rule could freeze them all *relatively* as they all rose uniformly.

With the introduction of the freeze on August 15, 1971, an especially loud complaint was heard about the abrogation of agreements made before the freeze for wage increases to be started after this date. It was claimed with great righteous indignation that to prevent the agreed-upon wage increases from taking place would be to go against the sacred principle of the validity and enforceability of contracts freely agreed upon. This sounds like a serious objection. Sacred or not, modern society could not exist without the maintenance of contracts. But there is an equally strong argument on the other side.

To the extent that the agreed-upon price increases were based upon the implicit acceptance by both parties of the expectation of inflation, which these increases were designed to offset, the freeze, by stopping the inflation, removes a basic assumption or implied condition of the contract. To insist on the contract's being carried out is like insisting upon being paid for a product which one has in fact not delivered or being compensated for damage which in fact has not been suffered.

Because of initial injustices and cumulative inefficiencies a freeze, just like the relative freezing of wages, cannot last very long. Flexibility has to be introduced, and that was the task of Phase Two of President Nixon's New Economic Policy.

Ideally, Phase Two would introduce just that flexibility that was missing in the wage-price guideposts that concentrated on stability. It would see that wages on the average must rise at a rate that corresponds to the target rate of inflation, but some wages must rise relative to others. Wages must rise more where labor is relatively tight, and less where labor is relatively plentiful. This is necessary first of all in order to prevent Phase Two from degenerating into real price control in those parts of the economy in which labor becomes more scarce. The market would then, as it were, be telling prices or wages to rise by more than that permitted by Phase Two. The whole plan would then break down in exactly the same way as the wage-price guideposts broke down.

Apart from the danger of a breakdown, flexibility or differential treatment of different kinds of wages in different parts of the economy is necessary to enable the market mechanism to perform its function of guiding the direction of resources and the production of different products in accordance with peoples' preferences and the conditions of production as these change over time. On the price side the function of Phase Two is to see to it that prices remain in normal relationship to costs. Prices must rise only in proportion to costs, and fall where costs fall.

Different rates of productivity increase in different parts of the economy (and in some parts of the economy there may well be productivity decreases), would require differential rates of price increases: smaller price increases or price decreases where there is a greater increase in productivity, and larger price increases where there is a smaller increase in productivity.

Phase Two has to learn to master the art of incomes policy regulation even while more and more groups in the economy will be trying to modify it, to water it down, to reduce it to impotence—or even plotting its outright abolition. Many will even be seeking its prenatal abortion—the abolition of the freeze before Phase Two is started. The question is: Can anything be done to increase the robustness of an incomes policy against all these attacks while it is still in an undeveloped condition? We turn to this problem in the next chapter.

Chapter 13

INSTANT PROSPERITY

WHILE a freeze can stop inflation in its tracks, it is not really a solution. As the very name implies, it is only a holding operation. It gives some time for something else to be done which could be a solution. Meanwhile time will run out. This is true not merely in the sense of the approaching date on which the freeze is declared to expire. If it is deemed necessary for the health of the economy, the freeze can no doubt be extended for another term or two. Time runs out because the accumulated feelings of injustice and the growing frustrations caused by its rigidity will lead to more and more exceptions being granted until the freeze disappears.

Developing and applying a genuine solution for the inflation is the task of Phase Two that follows the freeze. This means, first of all, setting up the principles and manner of administration of an incomes policy, while the freeze proper is in operation; and then a longer period of experimental application of the incomes policy itself until very many bugs have been removed, and difficulties ironed out. All this while we have the continuing irritations of the inevitable injustices of the initial application of the freeze, the growing inefficiencies due to the continuing rigidity of the whole pricing system under the freeze, and the imperfections of the fledgling incomes policy still finding its feet. The danger is that the resistances, objections, frustrations and dissatisfactions with the freeze and with the developing incomes policy, could lead to the melting of the freeze, the abrogation of the incomes policy, or its emasculation through the multiplication of exceptions, until it is all destroyed and the inflation comes back into power, trying to make up for lost time.

What is needed is some kind of counter pressure for the maintenance of the freeze and the protection of the developing incomes policy until it is strong enough to perform its task of controlling the inflation.

Fortunately there exists an almost ideal opportunity for providing such counter-pressures. There is something that can be done which would more than offset the resistance caused by the initial injustices and the growing economic inefficiencies. This is nothing more and nothing less than the removal of the inflationary depression.

That can be achieved by governmental monetary and fiscal policy—by a great increase in government spending or decrease in tax collections, or a combination of the two, involving a corresponding government deficit, helped along by an easing of credit and a corresponding increase in the quantity of money. The increased spending would result in an increase in output, employment, wages and profits. If it were seen that all these benefits were made possible by the freeze, those who gained from the prosperity, and those who sympathized with this alleviation of the suffering from the depression, would overwhelm the danger to the freeze from wholesale demands for "exceptions."

It is true that the same increase in total spending would have been possible quite apart from the freeze, and would have had the same effects on output, employment, profits and prosperity. But it could not be applied because of the generally and strongly held belief that any increase in total spending would accelerate inflation. With the establishment of the freeze, the argument loses its plausibility. As long as the freeze is in operation, it is not possible for inflation to accelerate or even to continue at the pre-freeze rate. Meanwhile the immediate benefits from "instant prosperity," would give the necessary lease of life to the freeze required for the proper development of Phase Two with its promised softening of the rigidities of the freeze. The continuing injustices and the growing inefficiencies of the freeze are as nothing compared with the increase in efficiency and justice, resulting from the reduction of unemployment from 6 per cent to 4 per cent with an increase in national output and income of some $70 billion a year.

Unfortunately, "instant prosperity" sounds too good to be true. So much so that the government has moved only very little in the direction of increasing total spending. It has promised to move further in this direction but only after a considerable and unnecessary delay.

In introducing the freeze President Nixon did speak about increasing total spending, and some of the tax reductions that he mentioned were directed toward this end. Unfortunately he could not escape from the sentiment—or maybe the political pressure—which called for reductions of expenditures at the same time in order to avoid an increasing deficit. This naturally worked in the opposite direction and frustrated the increase in demand, so that a possible mobilization of forces for maintaining the freeze and developing the incomes policy was not put into effect.

The basic reason for this failure to mobilize "instant prosperity" is the persistence of the belief that a greater government deficit is impermissible. Usually this is where the argument stops. If pressed to explain why it is impermissible, the opposition to "instant prosperity" falls back on the declaration that deficits cause inflation.

The persistence of this argument in conditions where the freeze has stopped the inflation is very difficult to explain. Part of it must be that economists have been much too successful over the last few hundred years in removing a number of medieval superstitions about inflation, in teaching how inflation is caused by too much spending, and in showing how too much spending has often been caused by government deficits and by money creation. There is not too much spending at the present time, as is clearly shown by the existence of several million workers who are unemployed because not enough money is being spent on the goods that they would be only too glad to produce. But this does not seem to register.

Government deficits *can* cause too much spending, and too much spending *does* cause inflation if prices are free to rise in response to too much spending. That does not mean, however, that deficits must cause inflation even if there is *too little* spending for prosperity and, because of the freeze, prices are *not free* to rise. Nevertheless, the same fear of government deficits which is responsible for our depression in the first place, the same wrongful application to conditions of too little spending of policies appropriate only for conditions of too much spending, has also prevented the increase in spending which could have brought about inflation-proof "instant prosperity" in the framework of the freeze.

And so we find ourselves with the possibility that the freeze and the incomes policy of Phase Two will peter out prematurely because the opportunity for "instant prosperity" was not seized, and that inflation will resume its pace with renewed energy. Moreover, as a result of attempts to moderate inflation by holding a tighter and tighter rein on total spending, we may also get to suffer from more and more severe depression.

Price control and repressed inflation consist of trying to prevent prices from rising when there is excess demand. But the essence of our problem is that we have prices rising *without* the existence of excess demand. There is therefore not the same reason why price control must break down. The purpose of incomes policy is *not* to prevent prices from rising in a free market where they have to rise because people are trying to buy more than there is. There is not in our case the shortage which must lead to the breakdown of price control or of repressed inflation. The argument is not applicable to a freeze or incomes policy undertaken to deal with Inflation III. Only in the case of Inflation I with excess demand, when the economy has reached a position of full employment and when such a shortage emerges, does the argument apply. In that situation it is indeed of the utmost importance, since it is certainly no better to treat Inflation I as if it were Inflation III than to treat Inflation III as if it were Inflation I.

Chapter 14

PHASE TWO

P HASE Two, as actually introduced and administered, was essentially the introduction, development, and application of the incomes policy for curing the economy of an inflation which we discussed in earlier chapters. It did not consist of a gradual disinflation by the device of providing a less than complete cost of living allowance, as described above in Chapter 11. Nor was it the complete price stabilizing incomes policy described in Chapters 8 and 9, which would have average wages increasing at a rate just equal to the increase in productivity. It was the second part of the two-phase alternative to the gradual disinflation device of Chapter 11, designed to follow after the first part—an over-all wage and price freeze. It consisted fundamentally of gradually bringing in the flexibility needed by any anti-inflation measure if it is to last over any period. It therefore had to concentrate on bringing the increase in wages relative to prices which is possible and necessary because of increasing productivity, and which also was put into cold storage in the introductory freeze.

Phase Two came into effect under difficult conditions be-cause of the failure of the government to carry out the policy of "instant prosperity" hinted at in the announcement of the New Economic Policy. Such an "instant prosperity" could have mobilized great forces to overcome resistance to the freeze and to the initial workings of the incomes policy. It was also handicapped by another kind of timidity, somewhat related to the timidity which prevented instant prosperity in spite of President Nixon's promise of increases in employment. These promises were themselves rather timid. They consisted of measures which might have increased total spending by some 5 billion dollars per annum, but these were to be applied gradually so as not to come into operation fully for a couple of years. At the same time a number of counter-measures were undertaken for the sake of serving the opposite objective of balancing the budget, and these had the effect of almost cancelling the promised expansionary effects. Parallel to this timidity was the decision not to try for price stability, but only for a moderation of inflation—to bring it down to a rate of some 2½% a year instead of all the way down to 0%.

There are probably many more respectable justifications for this than simply calling it timidity. Because of the incomplete success of the freeze there had been established not an expectation of stable prices but only an expectation of a somewhat slower rate of inflation. Many of the decisions on prices and wages encountered group pressures which were too powerful to be overcome. However, Phase Two was successful in bringing in flexibility and adjustments for increasing productivity and brought the rate of inflation down from 6% to 3½%. It should be possible to repeat the operation again and ultimately to reach the ideal zero rate of inflation, although there are some considerations which will make such repetitions more difficult. It would, for example, not be possible to exploit the crisis of an international balance of payments problem again.

Phase Two therefore had to adjust the incomes policy measures to a target rate of inflation of 2½%. As indicated before, this would mean that the average rate of increase of wages should be about 5½%, to allow for the 3% increase in productivity. As has already been explained above, there was a danger that this 5½% would become an overall and uniform rule, with exceptions only for cases of overwhelming pressure by the public or by particular groups. What is desirable for a successful incomes policy is, of course, not giving in to particular groups, but *appropriate* departures from the 5½% average rate—wages rising by more than the average in areas where the degree of unemployment is considerably less than the national average, and the opposite where there is more unemployment than on the average, rather than inappropriate departures from the average in response to economic and political pressures.

Fortunately appropriateness, from the point of view of efficiency in terms of the flexibility of the price mechanism under incomes policy, happens to fit in very closely with fairness with respect to relative wages, as we have seen above. It is fair that wages should be raised more where there is less unemployment, because the lower degree of unemployment is an indication that conditions in that part of the economy have not been attractive enough to induce many people to come into that area. Conversely, in areas where there is much more unemployment than the national average, it is fair that wages there should not rise as rapidly as elsewhere, because the high percentage of unemployment is an indication that many people prefer to stay there even though their chances of getting work are small. They must prefer to stay there because they consider that when they do get a job, it will more than make up for the waiting period.

Fairness, however, does not consist only of the relationship among different wage rates. There is also the question of the

113

relationship between wages and profits, and here it will appear to many that the incomes policy is not fair, but *biased* in the difference between the way it determines wages and the way it determines prices. The declared objective of Phase Two was indeed symmetrical. It aimed at wages rising on the average at $5\frac{1}{2}\%$, and prices rising on the average at $2\frac{1}{2}\%$, and this would allow everybody to enjoy the same 3% increase in real income.

The pure theory of incomes policy does not call for any regulation at all of profits as such, but only the maintenance of a normal degree of markup of price over costs, so that prices would remain in the same proportion to costs. If wages rise at $5\frac{1}{2}\%$, this would keep costs from rising more than $2\frac{1}{2}\%$ (because of the 3% increase in productivity). Prices would then be kept from rising more than $2\frac{1}{2}\%$ and everything would be perfectly fair. The share of profits, like the share of wages, would remain the same until this division between wages and profits was changed by something else. Nevertheless, the failure to regulate profits as such would seem unfair to many —and this feeling is easily exploited by politicians who will declare the whole device to be a fraud and a swindle on behalf of the capitalists.

All this is built on a basic misunderstanding. The proper parallel is not between wages and profits, but between wages and prices, between the price of labor, which is basically the price for inputs, and the price of final product—the price of outputs. What is needed for the success of an incomes policy is that the rate of markup—what is added to the cost in setting the price, out of which come the profits—should not be distorted. The rate of markup cannot be reduced very much without bringing many firms to bankruptcy. Nor should it be increased. Employers must not be allowed to use the incomes policy to increase their share of the national income.

If the rate of markup is maintained the shares will stay the same. If the cost per unit increases by 2½% the price will be increased by 2½% and the profit per unit will also increase by 2½%. But since there is a 2½% increase in the prices there will be no increase in the *real* profit per unit of output, while the worker, with his 5½% money wage increase is enjoying a 3% *real* increase. This does not mean that the capitalist has been cheated. We have not yet taken into account the increase in output, the increase in the number of units produced which is the other side of the increasing productivity. There will be 3% more units sold and therefore the total profit will increase by 3% too—the same as the increase in the real income of the workers. The 3% increase in productivity means that there is enough more produced for a 3% increase for everybody. The point that needs to be stressed here is that although the wage increases are determined by the rules (which fix them at 5½% on the average), prices are left for the market to determine. But in general the market will maintain the same markup as before for the very same reasons as before. Employers would always have liked a larger share (as indeed would the workers, or anybody else). But they have been limited by the previous markup which was determined by the existing *degree of competition,* or if one prefers to put it the other way round, by the *degree of monopoly* they had been able to establish. (The difference between these two is like the difference between a glass half full of water, and a glass which is half empty). With no change in the markup rate there will be no change in the share going to profit.

If the administered depression can be removed, there will indeed be an increase in profits. There will still be the same real profit per unit, but now the number of units on which the same profit is earned will increase not only by the 3%

increase in output per man employed, but also on account of the greater number of people employed as prosperity is reestablished. But this also is not in any way unfair, since there will be the same increase in the wages earned. As output increases when more people are employed, there is an increase in the wage bill—even though this increase in output does not raise the wage per unit or the wage per man—and there is a similar increase in total profits without any increase in profit per unit or profit per worker employed. This may be called an increase in the *profit bill* since it is exactly symmetrical to the increase in the wage bill. Total profits and total wages increase together, while the profits per unit of product and the wages per man stay the same.

However, this is true only of *gross* profit, not of *net* profit. Net profit is less than gross profit by the subtraction from the gross profit of the total fixed costs of business—those that do not vary with changes in output. The absolute changes in net profit are the same as the absolute changes in gross profit. For every billion dollars increase in gross profit there will be exactly a one billion dollars increase in net profit. But net profit is figured on a smaller base—smaller by the subtraction of the fixed costs from the total profit. The *percentage* increase in net profit would therefore be greater than the percentage increase in gross profit, and therefore also greater than the percentage increase in the wage bill. As output is increased the percentage or share going to *net profit* will increase and the percentage or share going to wages will have to diminish since they always add up to exactly 100%.

There is no doubt that this will be seized upon by the representatives of labor to show that an inequitable redistribution had occurred, that the capitalists are now gaining at the expense of the workers. They will not be able to say that the workers are being impoverished, since this redistribution occurs only when the wage bill is also being increased by the increase in output, employment and prosperity. But when we do have an increase in prosperity total net profits increase at a greater rate than total wages, and the *profit rate* increases relative to the *wage rate.*

This phenomenon is an inevitable result of any system in which workers are paid wages, even if it should be a completely socialist society. It would disappear only in an economy where the workers are paid not wages but only a fraction of the profits. Wherever workers are paid *wages,* whether in capitalist or in socialist societies, *profits*—what is left over after wages and other costs are met—is more variable than wages. This can also be put the other way round. Wages are more stable than profits.

The essence of the wage arrangement is that the workers are protected from the fluctuations in the earnings of the business. When business improves wages do not rise as much as profits. This is an inevitable recompense for arranging that the wages should not fall as much as profits do when business falls off. Profits quite often fall very much. They even become negative. Wages do not become negative. The essential condition of wages never falling so much is that they do not increase as much when the movement is in the opposite direction. Again it must be noted that all this applies even though there is no change in the rate of markup of the price over the costs.

It may very well be held desirable for the share going to wages to be greater than it is, and not only when the share of wages becomes smaller in times of prosperity. This very often takes the form of demanding larger money wage increases. When economists do not support such demands, they are often accused of being enemies of labor. But the reason for their not supporting such demands is because they are friends and wish to warn labor against the fallacy of expecting that such increases in money wages will increase the *real* share that labor gets. It cannot possibly do so as long as employers are free to make the normal adjustment of their markup in proportion to costs. This completely negates any expected benefits from increasing the money wage rate. Indeed, it is just this illusion which we wish to eliminate in trying to stop inflation. Excessive increases in money wages have the effect not of increasing the share going to labor, but only of increasing inflation.

This must not be understood as denying that a particular *group* of workers, as distinct from labor as a whole, can increase their real wage by raising their money wage. This will work as long as what they buy rises in price less than what they produce. This will be the case if other workers do not get corresponding increases in *their* wages, and for them what they buy will go up more than their wage. The first group will have gained not at the expense of their employers (who are protected by their rate of markup) but at the expense of the consumers of their product—primarily the other workers— and at the expense of those thrown out of work (in the first group) as less is bought of the product at the higher price, and fewer workers are needed to produce the smaller output.

There is indeed one way in which increasing money wages does lead to an increase in the percentage going to labor as a whole. This is when the increase in wages causes an increase in prices—i.e., an administered inflation, and attempts are made to stop the inflation by holding down the total rate of spending —i.e., by treating Inflation III as if it were Inflation I. In the resulting depression profits will fall more than wages, and so the share going to labor will increase.

It will be a larger percentage of a smaller income, and a

smaller share in absolute terms. It will be satisfactory to those, usually not workers, who are much more concerned about profits being less than they are concerned about wages being more, including any workers who are willing to accept a reduction in the wage bill for the satisfaction of knowing that there has been a larger reduction in profits. The economists who argue against excessive increases in money wages are not arguing against *improving* the condition of labor. They are arguing against the *mistake* of assuming that such excessive increases in money wages will improve the condition of the workers as a whole.

There are ways in which the condition of the poor, which includes many workers, really *can* be improved. It can be improve by a different system of taxation which will tax the richer more and the poorer less, although effects of this on efficiency and therefore on the total amount of income to be divided must also be taken into account. A different or better collection of taxes with less opportunity for rich men to take advantage of loopholes would help as would a greater degree of taxation of inheritance. Probably more important than this is the subsidization of education so as to enable workers to acquire useful and profitable skills. Still more important is the improvement of competition and the removal of resistance to entry into industries by competitors who would push down the rate of markup. Perhaps most important of all is exactly what we are concerned with in this book—namely the maintenance of full employment. Nothing does more to improve the income of a worker than to be employed instead of unemployed. Furthermore, with high employment the managers of industry have to pay much more attention to finding workers and keeping them, by providing conditions which will satisfy them rather than concentrating most of their energies on trying to persuade customers to buy. And finally, the continuation of a condition of full employment will make business so much more profitable as to induce more competition—providing this is not prevented by conspiracies, restrictions, monopolies of various kinds. The greater probability of larger sales would mean that the same return on capital invested can be expected from a smaller markup. This is a reflection of the same phenomenon which we have just been observing—the greater volatility of profits, as compared with wages. If employment should stay high and establish an expectation of its continuing to stay high, this will lead to greater competition resulting in a smaller markup, made up for by larger average sales volumes. The smaller markup is what increases the share going to labor of a *larger* total output.

On January 11, 1973, the government declared a change from Phase Two to "Phase Three." It may be little more than a change in name. The same wage and price restraints were to continue, with less emphasis on some parts of the economy and more on others. "Mandatory," but negotiable, controls were abolished, but there were threats of their reactivation if satisfactory "voluntary" restraints were not forthcoming. The declaration of "Phase Three" and the administrative changes may well make the incomes policy more effective. But if the "voluntary" restraints are not forthcoming, then the announced "Phase Three" will in effect be a return to "Phase Zero," where we were before August 15, 1971. In either case the announced "Phase Three" is not the Phase Three discussed in the next chapter. That can emerge only with the successful completion of the task of Phase Two: restoring a stable price level or at least stabilizing the inflation at an acceptable level so that there is no longer any danger of relapsing into a cure by depression.

120

Chapter 15

PHASE THREE

E VEN a completely successful incomes policy with the proper flexibility, undisturbed by pressure groups, is only a crude imitation of a properly working competitive market system. It cannot deal with different conditions in millions of points in the economy where the market mechanism would have served very much better to reflect changes in local conditions of demand, supply or technology. But the waste from such crudity of the substitute market mechanism is much less than the waste of unemployment, and maybe even less than the waste from continuing inflation, provided some protection is given to those who are hurt most severely by inflation. The justification of an incomes policy is essentially that it permits the elimination of administered depression and makes possible a functional finance policy of high or full employment.

The application of incomes policy is, of course, most inefficient in the beginning, but as the incomes policy continues to be applied—whether it is suddenly rechristened Phase Three or given any other name—it can do better and better. It develops into something somewhat closer to the market mechanism of classical economics.

This is due only in part to the development of criteria for determining when wages should rise more and when they should rise less than the average, and to the development of protection of the markup from exploitation by firms or industries which may find their monopoly power increased. As the expectation of inflation diminishes, the pressures which the incomes policy has to combat become weaker and weaker. More and more prices and wage rates are set by the market mechanism or by the wage and price administrators at levels which are not in conflict with the incomes policy. Phase Two becomes less and less active because it becomes less and less needed. What I am now describing is a kind of fading away of Phase Two with the elimination of the expectation of inflation on which Inflation III was based.

There are those who exaggerate the advantages of a truly free market by saying that it is infinitely better. Infinity, however, is a very large number. Suffice it to say that a free market is very much to be preferred, wherever it would work properly, to the administrative mechanisms of incomes policy in Phase Two. If the expectation of inflation should be replaced by an expectation of stable prices, Phase Two would atrophy. There would remain only the rudiments, the empty regulations which would not need to be put into action unless there should be a resurgence of a new inflation to be followed by a new freeze and a new incomes policy under a new Phase Two, which might once more fade away as it succeeded in removing the expectation of inflation.

There could thus be established a kind of psychological-political-economic cycle. This cycle, like all other cycles, can be made unnecessary if it is understood. The proper steps can be taken to prevent it rather than to cure it by avoiding the policies which would start it. In many cases this would merely mean the application of functional finance to prevent the excess demand of Inflation I. There are, of course, other possible igniters of expectations of rising prices. But whatever it was that started an Inflation III, the removal of the expectation of rising prices by an incomes policy would lead to a return to the much more efficient and much more satisfactory free market mechanism. This is what I am calling Phase Three.

There has been much opposition to Phase Two by economists and even more by moralists with a completely different argument. They refer to the damage done to society by having laws to regulate wages and prices, declaring that such laws are bound to break down, to fail to be respected, and this will lead to the decay of respect for law and great damage to the whole moral climate of society. There can be no question that for all sorts of reasons which we can not go into here, there has been a deterioration in the respect for law, and an increase in crime. But to blame Phase Two, or incomes policy, for significantly contributing to the loss of a respect for law rests on a mistaken identity—exactly the opposite of the mistaken identity discussed in an earlier chapter. There we spoke of the evils which resulted from treating Inflation II as if it were Inflation I, trying to stop inflation caused by wage and price administrators as if it were inflation due to too much spending. We saw that this mistaken identity led to holding down total spending as a cure for Inflation II or Inflation III. This, being the wrong remedy, did not cure inflation, but instead presented us with administered depression. The mistake in the present case is exactly the reverse. The cure for Inflation III is declared to be inappropriate because of the harm it would do if used as a cure for Inflation I. The mistake here is not in applying the wrong remedy. Based on the same confusion, it consists of *refusing to use the right remedy*. It is, of course, not possible to cure Inflation I by an incomes policy. If there is too much spending any attempt at regulating prices or wages could lead only to repressed inflation with all its moral evils. But since the regulations of incomes policy are to be applied only as long as there is *not* too much spending, and only when the wage and price administrators are pushing up prices *against* the market, none of these horrors are real. They are fantasies born of the same mistaken identity when approached from the other side.

If incomes policy succeeds in stopping rising prices and, after a time, removing the *expectation* of rising prices, the managers of Phase Two find themselves with less and less to do as we move toward Phase Three. This is the turn from Inflation III to Inflation 0—the situation where prices are not rising, and are not expected to be rising. The defensive expectational Inflation III loses the basis on which it stands. We can have price stability with full employment and without any further active operation of Phase Two's incomes policy. In Phase Three we are back again in the natural healthy situation of prosperity without any administered inflation or wage and price administrators that need regulating. There would only be the frame-work of the incomes policy for re-activation if it should ever become necessary.

This happy ending to the story, however, will not emerge if it should turn out that we had to deal not with Inflation III but with Inflation II. As long as the different parties to production are insisting on getting more than 100% of the product between them, this will not work. Inflation II can be stopped only by bringing about sufficient depression to crush the insistence of the parties on shares adding up to more than the whole product.

It was with such a theoretical "solution" in mind that I distinguished between high full employment and low full employment when I wrote *The Economics of Employment* back in 1951. High full employment was what one would naturally call full employment, when all who wanted to work were able to work as much as they wished to at the current wages. Unemployment would be only of the frictional type, involving people who were on their way from one job to another, or who were temporarily unemployed because their skills were inappropriate or they were in the wrong part of the country. Low full employment would be that level of employment at which prices were stable. But this would mean that Inflation II pressures for increasing wages and prices had been liquidated by a long, severe and continuing depression.

The only excuse I can give for calling this any kind of full employment, is that I had not at the time realized that this was a basic departure from the Keynesian view in which both of these "full employments" were regarded as identical. It had assumed that the right amount of spending is all that is needed for "flation"—neither inflation nor depression. In this language this would mean that low full employment, which is required for price stability, and which I at that time described as corresponding to 6 million unemployed in the United States, is identical with high full employment, with only frictional type unemployment, which I described as corresponding to 2 million unemployed in the United States. It is the failure to see the existence, or even the possibility, of this gap which constitutes the inadequacy of the Keynesian theory of inflation and depression and of the functional finance policies for dealing with these problems.

The Phillips curve, of which we have been hearing a great deal in recent years, is a refinement of what seems to be the same idea as the distinction between high full employment and low full employment. It is a much more sophisticated idea since it consists not of two points but of a curve which contains all the combinations of degrees of employment (or unemployment) and corresponding degrees of inflation between high full employment and low full employment. Each possible combination of unemployment and inflation is represented by a point on a curve anchored on the two limiting positions: high full employment with the highest level of inflation considered and only frictional unemployment, and low full employment with the highest level of unemployment considered and no inflation at all.

The Phillips curve suggests that we have the possibility of choosing where we would like to be on that curve; whether we would rather have more unemployment and less inflation, or less unemployment and more inflation. As indicated above, the evil from 1% more unemployment is so much greater than the evil from 1% more inflation that if one has a choice in this trade off one should always choose a point nearer high full employment, the upper end of the Phillips' curve, where there is less unemployment even if this means more inflation.

It is, however, questionable whether we really can obtain higher levels of employment at the cost of higher levels of inflation, or lower levels of inflation at the cost of lower levels of employment. We can get higher or lower levels of *employment* by providing higher or lower levels of spending, but between the politically and morally impermissible catastrophic depression that crushes Inflation II, and the excessive demand of Inflation I, the effects on *prices* and inflation are questionable. Neither a lower nor a higher level of employment makes it possible for the sellers to get more than 100% of the product. But in the absence of an incomes policy, *any* level of employ-

126

ment, in conjunction with Inflation II, will be accompanied by continuing and accelerating administered inflation of wages and prices. The resistance to the greater inflation, taking the form of monetary restraint, will restore the previous politically determined level of administered depression.

The argument (which will be recognized as similar to Professor Milton Friedman's "natural level of employment") is stronger than might seem from this formulation. It applies not only to any attempt to *increase* the level of employment at the cost of an *increase in the rate* of inflation, but also to attempts to *maintain*, at any *level of* inflation, any level of employment greater than the politically determined inflationary recession. Even with much unemployment, however, as long as there is any inflation going on, rising prices will be blamed by labor and capital for the failure of attempts to obtain more than 100% of the product, and the same escalation of inflation will result. Only at the level of low full employment—the zero point on the Phillips curve—will we be able to achieve Milton Friedman's natural level of employment. This means a degree of unemployment and of business depression severe enough (and long-lasting enough) to have destroyed the power of the wage administrators to raise wages by more than the increase in productivity.

In Professor Friedman's formulation, any rate of employment greater than his natural rate of employment results in inflation, and any rate of employment below his natural rate leads to deflation. The result is that total money spending at any given level will lose purchasing power in the inflation case, and will gain purchasing power in the deflation case, automatically restoring employment to his natural level, no matter what the level of total spending. If total spending is increased in proportion to the increase in output, the 4 per cent or so a year that shows the combination of the increase in output per worker and the increase in the number of workers, we will have neither inflation nor deflation, but price stability—with, of course, his "natural" level of employment. This looks somewhat like Functional Finance or Keynesian economics, but it is only the price level that is controlled by this "right amount of spending" and not the level of employment.

Professor Friedman's analysis also looks very much like the classical analysis in his system's inability to provide more than a natural rate of employment (except for temporary periods when workers are misled by inflation into believing that they are getting more than they really are). The analysis suggests that the additional workers (those employed only when the level of employment is above his natural rate) do not really want to work for the real wage they can get. They are *voluntarily* unemployed (except during the inflations when they are *involuntarily employed;* they are enslaved—not indeed by force, but by the fraud of the inflation).

This fits in with Professor Friedman's known adherence to the "objective" methodology that considers only "revealed preferences." The workers who are unemployed at the natural level of employment (my "low full employment") are seen as acting "as if" they did not want to work at the prevailing real wage.

Whenever they are employed (which is only when employment is above the "natural" level) money wages rise. It is "as if" instead of being pleased at having found work they felt cheated and were insisting on a higher rate of pay if they are to continue to come to work. But there are those who, like myself, find it possible to distinguish between the wage administrators (even if these reflect a policy supported by a majority vote of the workers) and the newly employed and unemployed men and women. The decisions of the wage administrators (which are the revelations from which the "revealed preferences" are derived) are not necessarily the true preferences of the newly employed men and women who usually do not say that they are sorry they went to work, or of the unemployed who would be willing to take jobs at the current wage (or even less), but have not been able to find them. To these the "natural" level of employment is still a "low full employment" which does not really deserve to be called full employment. It is only the depression position that would be reached by the consistent treatment of Inflation II with the remedy appropriate for Inflation I, if any government were callous enough, fanatical enough, and suicidal enough to persist in such a policy to the bitter end.

But the zero point on the Phillips curve (which is identical with my "low full employment") still does not really mean no inflation. It only means no *unexpected* inflation. Any excess of inflation over and above that expected would cause capital and labor to respond by increasing their claims. If there is no unexpected inflation, the claims for higher wages or higher prices remain unchanged, and the expected degree of inflation or of acceleration of inflation comes about as anticipated. The expectation of stable prices, namely, an expectation of a zero rate of inflation, is only a special case. The zero point on the Phillips curve, or "low full employment," represents a situation in which the expectations, whatever they might be, could be realized. A higher level of employment would bring about higher inflation than that anticipated or expected. And a lower level of employment would result in a rate of inflation (or of acceleration of inflation) lower than that anticipated. Even "low full employment" is no unfailing specific against Inflation III.

This is a misleading symmetry, however. It is not the symmetry between excess demand and deficient demand. Deficiency of demand is operative when there is less than *low* full employment, but above this level it is not excess demand but pressure by sellers that raises prices and price expectations. Only when there is more than *high* full employment does excess demand come into play, and then incomes policy cannot work. Attempts to apply it would result only in price control, with all its evils and inevitable breakdown.

In the range between high full employment (say 3% unemployment) and low full employment (say 10 or 15% unemployment) it is possible for incomes policy to stabilize the degree of actual, and thereby of expected, inflation, making the two equal. This *flattens out this portion of the Phillips curve*, as shown in the accompanying simple diagram. The level of unemployment (U) measures, from left to right, how low the economy is running. Vertically is measured the excess of actual inflation (AI) over expected inflation (EI). H indicates high full employment, and L low full employment.

To the left of H we have excess demand, overfull employment, and Inflation I. The farther to the left, the greater the excess demand, the overemployment, the excess of actual over expected inflation, and the inflationary pressure. In this region dwells the dragon of hyperinflation. To the right of L we have so severe a deficiency of demand that unemployment and depression have broken the power of workers and of business to press for higher wages and prices. There is no Inflation II or Inflation III to counter the downward market pressure on wages and prices, and we have deflation. Perhaps we should call this Deflation I, it being the obverse of Inflation I. In this region dwell the wild beasts of hyperdeflation.

The two tails of the diagram—the backward rising curve to

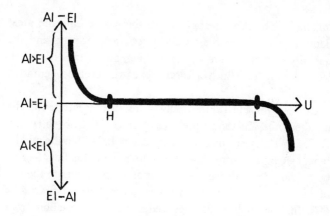

the left of H and the forward falling curve to the right of L—if put together, leaving out the middle range, exactly represent the classical theory of the price level, which failed to deal with depression. It failed because there is no "point" or knife-edge of a single "natural" or equilibrium level of employment at which the tails meet. Between the tails at the extremes there is the wide range that encompasses various degrees of depression or recession from high full employment to low full employment. Within this range much or little unemployment is compatible with much or little inflation, so that incomes policy can change the inflation rate, and aggregate spending policy (functional finance) can change the unemployment rate.

Some countries have for brief periods found themselves in hyperinflations of excess demand to which the tail on the left refers. So far no economy has found itself in a hyperdeflation (the right-hand tail) with prices falling more and more rapidly while the total quantity of money in the economy is continually being decreased the way it is continually increased in hyperinflations. The nearest approach to this was during the great depression of the thirties, when prices, employment, and the quantity of money were all diminishing, but there is no reason for believing that such a catastrophe will ever be permitted again.

Our present and future troubles are all concentrated in the middle range. Inflation I prevents us from going above H, and Deflation I prevents us from going below L. Within the middle range attempts during the 1960's to reduce Inflation I or II by holding down demand (for fear of slipping over to the left of H into hyperinflation) increased unemployment from 4 to 6%. Incomes policy then reduced the rate of inflation from 6 to 3½% per annum even while unemployment was reduced from 6 to 5%. If the unfulfillable ambitions of Inflation II can be stilled and the expectations that give rise to Inflation III can be eliminated by an uninhibited use of incomes policy, we will be able to apply the principles of functional finance in accordance with Keynes's economic policy to establish and maintain an optimal level of employment at a stable or even a zero rate of inflation.

Chapter 16

THE DOLLAR ABROAD:

I. How It Could Work

I T may seem strange that we have gone so far in this
book without mentioning gold or foreign exchange, especially as the New Economic Policy was apparently
triggered by a crisis in the relationship of the dollar to
gold and foreign currencies. The international aspects of the
dollar problem could be left to the end because international
trade is relatively unimportant for the U.S., and because the
same principles developed in earlier chapters for dealing with
domestic problems are immediately applicable to international
problems.

The importance for the U.S. of foreign trade, other foreign
economic transactions, and all the related problems is often
much exaggerated. They are of relatively small importance to
the United States because we are such a large country that
almost everything we need can be provided within our borders.

Our foreign trade, like that of any country, consists essentially
of producing goods for export to earn the foreign currencies
("foreign exchange") we pay for our imports. In our case
this comes to about 4%—one twenty-fifth—of the gross national product, or some $40 billion. Our exports generate a

supply of foreign currencies, the currencies supplied by foreigners to obtain the dollars to pay for our exports. (If they pay for them in foreign currencies it makes no difference, it only means that the exporter who gets them supplies them instead in exchange for the dollars he needs to run his business here.) The *demand* for foreign currencies is generated by our imports. We have to pay for the imports in foreign currencies. There are additional demands for and supplies of foreign currencies for other purposes, but we can treat all these as payments for additional imports or exports. All the dollar, gold and foreign currency crises arise from differences between the supply and the demand for foreign currencies.

Some of our imports are very difficult to produce domestically, and some even impossible. On the other hand, most of them could be produced here but only at a higher cost than the exports we produce to get the foreign exchange (the foreign currencies) with which we buy them. That is why it pays us to get them in this indirect way instead of producing them ourselves. We are relatively more efficient in producing our exports, and other countries are relatively more efficient in producing *their* exports (our imports).

We can figure about how "vital" it is for us to maintain our foreign trade by supposing that for some reason it was curtailed. If we had to give up half of it, we would export $20 billion less and import $20 billion less. We would be made worse off by this reduction in our foreign trade because making the imports ourselves (or adequate substitutes for them) would cost us more than making the exports we exchange for them. The degree of higher cost would vary. Let us suppose that it goes all the way up to twice as much (those imports which we cannot make ourselves, or would cost us more than twice as much to make ourselves, would be in the half of our trade which we would not give up). The loss from the higher cost would thus vary from zero for goods which are just worth importing to 100% on the most beneficial to us, where the loss is greatest. On the average the loss would be about half the value of the trade given up—about $10 billion.

That is a lot of money, but it is still only 1% of the gross national product, and therefore still minor in relation to our topic which is the size of the whole GNP. Furthermore, there is very little chance of such an enormous reduction in the amount of our trade even under the worst of reasonably conceivable circumstances; and for smaller reductions in trade the loss is much more than proportionately smaller. The loss varies as *the square* of the reduction in trade. Under the same assumptions, giving up 10% of our trade, a fifth as big a cut, would involve giving up only items where the greater cost of domestic production is not so much, varying from zero to 20%, averaging 10%; and it would apply to only $4 billion of trade. The loss would be only $0.4 billion, 0.04% of the GNP—only *one twenty-fifth* of the loss from giving up half of our foreign trade and only one twenty-five-hundreth of the GNP—an amount by which our GNP grows in about half a week!

The crisis which was the occasion for the New Economic Policy consisted of a "dollar glut." Central banks in Europe and Japan had accumulated a great quantity of United States dollars over a number of years during which our demand for foreign currencies (the supply of dollars) had been much greater than the supply of foreign currencies (the demand for dollars by foreigners to pay for their American imports). Some 16 billion of these dollars had been turned in to the United States in exchange for gold, so that our stock of gold fell from $26 billions' worth (at $35 an ounce) after World War II to about $10 billions' worth. Another $40 billion remained abroad, and its owners had the right to ship it back here in return for more gold than we had (at the $35 an ounce which we had guaranteed). The crisis consisted of this possibility being taken as a threat.

This threat has to be taken with several grains of salt since at the same time the central banks were complaining that they were *running short* of foreign exchange, which includes these dollars, and showed great concern at anything the United States might do that would slow down the flow of dollars they were acquiring. They needed them for their "liquidity." But we must leave that until later. The "dollar glut" stands in striking contrast to the opposite phenomenon—a "dollar shortage" which appeared during and after World War II. The two are closely related. During the war, our productive capacity had been vastly expanded even while we were providing our allies with military and other supplies. War finance had worked as a kind of unconscious functional finance, putting to work for these purposes the resources that had been unemployed during the preceding depression. Europe and Asia had meanwhile been devastated. The whole world needed to be rebuilt. For this they needed the goods which only we could provide on a large enough scale, and they did not have the dollars to buy them. That was the dollar shortage.

Over the years these countries were rebuilt, with a great deal of American aid, and no longer needed as much of our products. They had also modernized their equipment and were able to supply more and more goods to us. Consequently there was a turnaround. Our exports, which had been running as much as $7 billion a year in excess of our imports, fell relative to the imports until in 1972 imports exceeded exports by $6 billion. Meanwhile we were demanding as much as $7 billion worth a year of foreign currencies over and above the amounts needed to pay for our imports, to finance our foreign aid, for our investments and military expenditures abroad and a number of other items. The excess demand for foreign currencies was, of course, an excess supply of dollars in buying them. This was the dollar glut.

There is a natural and automatic cure for such situations in the classical, supply and demand, operation of any market. Excess demand is cured by a price increase and excess supply is cured by a price decrease. We have seen (Chapter 2) that if prices are prevented from rising when we have excess demand we get into the troubles caused by price control or repressed inflation. If prices do not fall when there is deficient demand we get unemployment. These problems do not arise if there is a well developed market mechanism and it is allowed to operate.

In the international money market—the foreign exchange market—where different national monies are exchanged for each other, we have perhaps the most perfect of all markets, with instant electronic communication over the whole world for perfectly standardized items (unlike, say, wheat for which there is an excellent international market in spite of the great variations in kinds and qualities). But *the market is not allowed to operate.* This is why we have the problems, the shortages and the gluts.

If the market had been allowed to operate freely after World War II, the excess demand for dollars would have raised the price of the dollar in terms of other currencies (i.e., lowered the prices of foreign currencies in terms of the dollar). At the higher price the demand for dollars would have been less. It would have been limited to demand by those who were not discouraged by the higher price. At the same time the supply of dollars would have been greater as Americans were induced to buy more imported goods, cheaper in terms of their (appreciated) dollars. There would have been no dollar shortage.

If the market had been allowed to operate in the last few years the excess demand for foreign currencies (the excess supply of dollars) would have raised the price of foreign currencies in terms of the dollar (i.e., lowered the price of the dollar in terms of the foreign currencies). This would have made our goods cheaper for foreigners (they could pay with cheaper dollars) and their goods dearer for us (we would have to pay in more expensive foreign currency). They would have imported more of our exports, *demanding more dollars* to pay for them. We would have imported less goods, *supplying fewer dollars* in exchange for foreign currencies to pay for these. There would be no dollar glut.

This is the heart of all the international monetary crisis problems. They are all the result of the market in national currencies not being allowed to perform its normal function of bringing supply and demand into equilibrium by adjusting the price. We now have to examine *the ways* in which we interfere to prevent the market from operating freely and *why* we do this. The second is more difficult to understand and the more interesting study. It will be left for the next chapter.

The interference does not in general take the form of crude price control—foreign exchange restrictions, ceilings on the price of foreign currencies, and prohibitions on trading except by specific permits. Where foreign exchange restrictions are imposed they lead to the same evasions and black markets and breakdowns as any other price controls, and most of the richer countries frown on such crude procedures.

The respectable way of preventing the market from doing its

job is by *pegging* the price. This means maintaining a price, not by prohibiting other prices, but by coming into the market as a residual buyer or seller at the chosen price and buying or selling enough of what is being bought and sold to swamp any potential excess of supply or of demand. In a sense, the market seems to be working. Everybody can buy or sell as much as he wants to. But changes in "regular" demand or supply have no effect on the price because the residual buyer-seller—the *pegger*—is *offsetting* any excess or deficiency of demand.

Such pegging is often done with commodities, like corn, in the name of stabilization. Anyone (government or private individual or group) can do this if he has large enough *stocks* of money and of the item and *if he is really concerned only with stabilization*. This means that he does not try to change the *average* level of the price but only to iron out *fluctuations* about the average or norm which it would have followed in any case. This activity is even profitable too, since it means preventing the price from moving much below the norm by buying only when the price has fallen below it, and preventing the price from rising much above the norm by selling only when it has risen above it. The same can also be done for the price of one currency in terms of another. For this, of course, one needs stocks of the two currencies large enough to be able to absorb temporary differences between demand and supply on the market. This activity, pegging, is undertaken by arbitrageurs and speculators for profit and by governmental "exchange stabilization funds" for stability.

Trouble arises when a pegger tries to maintain a price *which turns out not to be the norm*. He then finds that he has to keep on buying and runs out of money, or he finds he has to keep on selling and runs out of the commodity. In the case of "currency stabilization" he runs out of one or the other of the two currencies whose rate of exchange for each other he is pegging. His stocks are not big enough, he says. He may be thinking that the norm is still the same but that there has been an unusually large fluctuation—a temporary excess of supply or demand—and he cries for help, in the form of a *loan* of money (if he is buying) or of the commodity (if he is selling) or of the particular currency he is selling (if he is supplying it in exchange for another in a pegging operation). If he gets a loan he can continue for a while, but if the norm *has* changed, he will run out again. What he now needs is not a *stock* large enough to enable him to fill temporary and alternating excesses of demand and excesses of supply. What he now needs is a continuing *flow* of the appropriate loans. He may, for a time, be able to get more of such loans, but finally, when it becomes evident that the hole is bottomless, his credit will collapse and he will find himself in crisis. He may not wait until he has none left of the item he is selling, but stop when his remaining stock is too dangerously low. This only makes the crisis come sooner.

During the dollar shortage, the dollar was pegged at too low a price in terms of the other currencies, and was in great demand. The United States supplied dollars to meet this demand in the course of buying up gold, increasing the United States stock of gold to $26 billions' worth, about two-thirds of the world's monetary stock of gold. More billions of dollars were made available in gifts and loans. But all this was not enough to satisfy the demand for dollars. Direct price controls, i.e., currency controls, were also imposed in many countries and there was an administrative rationing of dollars by special permits—the symptom of dollar scarcity.

In recent years it was the other way around. The level at which the dollar was stabilized was now too high. This meant that dollars had to be bought to keep its price *up*. We bought $16 billion in selling that much gold. Some $40 billion were bought by central bankers throughout the world. This was still not enough, and in the last few years we imposed restrictions on the purchase of foreign currency for certain purposes. This again was a move from pegging the price to less conspicuous forms of direct price control as we saw ourselves running out of the means for continuing our pegging: the foreign currencies, the loans of foreign currencies and the gold for which we could get foreign currencies. On September 15, 1971, we decided to stop pegging. The dollar, of course, immediately floated downward because we had stopped the pegging operation that was keeping it higher than the norm.

Chapter 17

GOLD AS A WORLD MONEY

W E must now consider the mystery of why we go in for pegging rates of exchange, and even turn to direct currency controls when we run out of the foreign currencies needed for pegging, instead of letting the international money market work freely in the first place and automatically equalize the balance of payments between countries.

The story begins with the classical theory of the gold standard according to which all the money used in all the countries of the gold standard system consisted of gold, or else of notes representing gold which was locked up safely somewhere so that they were in effect "golden paper." The different currencies of the different countries were merely different denominations of corresponding quantities of gold, just as nickels, dimes, and silver dollars are all different denominations of the dollar. Just as the dollar is the United States' national money, gold was the world's money. The passion for "stabilizing" the prices of different currencies in terms of gold and consequently also in terms of each other, derives from a kind of idealization of this single world money, in a sentimental internationalism similar to the idealization of an imaginary distributist society referred to in Chapter 2.

The idealized gold standard theory of automatic equilibrium of international payments, like the classical automatic full employment theory discussed in Chapter 3, rests on the assumption of flexibility of wages and prices. If a country imports more than it exports (in value) it is a deficit country and must pay for the difference in gold, the universal or world money. Money therefore flows out of the country. It is the same if it pays in "golden paper" because the foreigners exchange the paper for the gold it represents, and take home the gold.

As the quantity of money in the deficit country diminishes, total spending is reduced (this is a converse of the business man's argument number three in Chapter 5) and prices and wages fall (by the axiom of flexibility). The deficit country's exports become cheaper and foreigners buy more. As the money supply in the other countries (the surplus countries) increases, total spending and wages and prices increase there. Their exports become more expensive and the deficit country imports less of them. The deficit country's exports rise and its imports fall until they become equal and the balance of payments problem automatically disappears.

The reader will notice the similarity between this procedure and the adjustment via flexible rates of exchange between currencies. Here we get the same results without having different currencies appreciating and depreciating in terms of each other. We see a beautiful, single world money with powerful appeal as a symbol of planetary unity—a "one world."

Unfortunately for this dream, as for the dream of classical automatic full employment, we just do not have the wage and price flexibility that it required for it to work. As we have seen, we would not get the *deflation* of wages and prices that would do the trick, but *depression,* or deflation of the economy, instead.

Strangely enough, this does not settle the matter because depression also does the trick after a fashion. The deficit country would import less because of the depression (while the opposite happens in the surplus countries) and this would automatically correct the deficit. This is clearly related to the "sound finance" policy that would cure domestic administered inflation by creating a sufficiently deep depression.

Here we would do well to remember Charles Lamb's essay on the discovery of roast pork, and the period before the invention of methods for roasting the pig without burning down the house. In the U.S. for example, since only about 4% of the income is spent on imports, to reduce imports by $1 billion the depression might have to reduce total income by $25 billion. The rejection of the classical (and functional finance) cure for demand inflation as a remedy for administered inflation represents rejection of a remedy similar to burning down the house to roast the pig. Modern societies have refused to apply the deep depression cure for administered inflation. In the same way they have refused to apply the depression cure for balance of payments deficits. In both cases this decision saved the house. The deep enough depression was avoided. But the pig, in both cases, did not get roasted. The inflation continued and gold kept flowing out of the deficit countries.

A balance of payments deficit country refuses to accept the domestic depression cure for the deficit by not permitting the outflow of gold to reduce the quantity of domestic money within the country. This means replacing the diminishing gold-money and golden-paper-money by issuing locally produced money *not* backed by gold, and constitutes a break with the gold standard as far as the domestic supply of money is concerned. A symmetrical break with the gold standard occurs in the balance of payments surplus countries which do not want the domestic supply of money to be increased by the *inflow* (possibly inflationary) of gold. Such countries withdraw domestic money from circulation (taxing or borrowing it without respending) to the degree necessary to prevent the domestic money supply from being increased by the inflow of gold. The gold inflow is thus *offset* and is said to be "sterilized."

But it is only *domestically* that the gold standard has been made completely inoperative. In international payments the chains have not been broken. The vision of a single world money for international payments has not lost its charm— or perhaps it would be better to say its spell has not been broken. It is generally described not as a single world money, but by its distinguishing feature—the fixity of the rates of exchange between the national monetary units. This fixity is maintained by pegging the different national monies in terms of each other.

A surplus country does not have any difficulty in maintaining the pegging because its currency tends to go *up* above the "fixed" rate. To prevent this, it has to *sell* its currency—buying other currencies with it. It can always continue with the pegging as long as it wants to because there is nothing to prevent it from printing as much of its domestic money as it may need. A deficit country's currency, however, tends to go *down*. To prevent this it has to *buy* its own currency with foreign currency— which it cannot just print. When it runs out of foreign currency (or of gold, or credit, which could provide it with more foreign currency) we have the crisis. The crisis could be cured by a fall in wages and prices, which does not happen, or by a depression which is rejected.

We have seen how administered inflations may be cured by

incomes policy which, if successful, permits functional finance to solve the domestic problems of inflation and depression. In the case of the balance of payments problem, no such new mechanisms are required—only the cessation of the pegging. The pegging would indeed be stopped perforce when there was no more foreign exchange left or when the country did not want to let its reserves drop any further. Such cessation of pegging was regarded not as a policy adopted by the country but as a catastrophe that had overtaken it—a bankruptcy that should be avoided or at least delayed as much as possible. Because it was something the country would be forced to in the end, it was hard to see that it was something that it should have welcomed in the beginning.

"Stability" is the *good* word for describing the fixity of an exchange rate maintained by pegging. The corresponding *bad* word with the same meaning is "rigidity." For the bad word "instability," the corresponding good word is "flexibility." Those who favor the policy of pegging the exchange rates, therefore sing the virtues of stability and order in a system of fixed exchange rates and see in the crisis only the unfortunate results of misbehavior by various culprits—and scapegoats are never too difficult to find. But in the absence of wage and price flexibility, the stability of the exchange rates means that there is no way left of adjusting to changes in the relative economic positions of the different countries. The change in the United States since World War II, starting as the only source for the reconstruction of a ruined world and then turning into a lagging member of a rapidly growing (developed) world, is only a rather dramatic example of changes which are always taking place. The change from dollar scarcity to dollar glut is evidence that the dollar was undervalued and became overvalued. If it had been more expensive and then became less expensive there would have been no dollar scarcity, no dollar glut, and no dollar crisis. But that would mean *flexibility* of the exchange rates which was, and largely still is, regarded as bad and therefore called *instability* or chaos or worse.

But the "stability" of exchange rates that was the official policy until August 15, 1971, was unmistakable rigidity in the exact sense of the word. It was an attempt to avoid inevitable adjustments and it inevitably failed to prevent them. It was able only to resist them temporarily—by pegging operations— until they built up sufficient pressure to break through the resistance. There was then a *large* change, a *devaluation* first of one currency and then of another in successive crises—Britain in 1931, the United States in 1933, France in 1936. Attempts to strengthen the system in 1936, and to reconstruct it in 1944, were followed by more devaluations in 1949. Then came a period of "stability" maintained by unprecedently large loans of the most varied and ingenious kind to help maintain record outlays on pegging until the system began to crack in 1967. We shall consider these events in the next chapter. Here we concentrate on showing how "stability" is really rigidity.

There is an almost perfect analogy to this in the physical nature of the California earthquakes. The San Andreas fault is a crack in the earth's surface that runs through San Francisco. Deep earth movements are constantly shifting one side relative to the other, but the rocks on both sides of the crack are pressed together hard and catch against each other so that they resist the movement at the crack while the masses of rock away from the crack continue to move. The rock twists and the pressure at the crack builds up. Any day now, geologists tell us, the resistance will be overcome. There will be a sudden large earth movement and a possible repetition of the disastrous 1907 San Francisco earthquake. If the rocks at the crack had not

148

caught and meshed against each other, if they had smooth surfaces that could glide, there would be a small, even imperceptible, gradual movement in adjustment to the underlying forces. But the rocks do catch against each other and so we have the same kind of "stability" as is provided by the system of pegged exchange rates. That system may be called "fixed" exchange rates, but the fixity cannot prevent the adjustments in the exchange rates to changing world economic conditions. It can only resist the adjustment until the pressure built up overcomes the resistance. The result is an alternation of rigidity and crises.

The system of pegged exchange rates finds much support, in addition to the ideological attractions of sentimental internationalism, from practical businessmen who claim that the stability of exchange rates is a great convenience for international trade and other international economic transactions. It saves them from having to worry about the value in domestic money of payments they will receive, or will have to make, in the future in foreign currencies.

This is perfectly understandable from businessmen who may never have experienced a devaluation and who tend to believe that the stability is really forever. They are also prone to imagine that the small and gradual movements in unpegged exchange rates, as conditions gradually change, would be like the large devaluations which take place when the pegging of an exchange rate is finally overcome by the accumulated pressures that had built up. Furthermore, it is natural for non-economists not to see that the same underlying forces which ultimately lead to the abandonment of the "fixed" rate of exchange are still operating all the time while the "fixed" rate of exchange is preventing the adjustment of the balance of payments. The authorities will try to take other steps to achieve this adjustment, i.e., by restrictions of imports, by tariffs, quotas, subsidies to import substitutes, or by exchange restrictions. These actions will hamper imports (about which the businessmen are concerned) just as much, without at the same time encouraging exports (which is what would simultaneously be done by the normal downward adjustment of the deficit country's exchange rate) so that there will be in addition a general reduction in trade in mutual "beggar-thy-neighbor" activities that result from this misguided "internationalism."

It will be noticed that in the course of this discussion gold came to play a secondary role. The essence is the pegging of the rates of exchange between the *currencies* of the different countries, not whether gold plays any part in the procedure by which the rates of exchange are kept fixed. What matters for international trade is the rate of exchange between, say, the Dollar and the Yen, the price of these in terms of each other, since this is what determines what imports and exports are profitable. The prices of the currencies in terms of gold are nothing more than the inverse of the price of gold in terms of the currencies. Nevertheless, the price of gold still plays a great part in the current problems, even though mostly as a historical-psychological hangover from past ages when different national currencies were nothing more than certain weights of gold. Since 1944, the different currencies have been related to a certain weight of gold only indirectly, namely, by being pegged to the U.S. dollar, which in turn was pegged to gold. Nevertheless, in recent negotiations on how much the dollar should depreciate in terms of other currencies, a sticking point in the negotiations was how much of this should be in terms of the depreciation of the dollar in terms of gold and how much should be in terms of the appreciation of other currencies in terms of gold.

It would seem that the French government insists on preventing the franc from appreciating in terms of gold by having the price of gold raised to the same degree as the franc in terms of the dollar. By these means she will be able to deny responsibility for the appreciation of the franc in terms of the dollar, which impairs the competitiveness of French exporters, and avoid having the price of gold falling in terms of the franc and upsetting her gold-hoarding peasants and bankers. But apart from such political semantics the position of the line drawn between appreciation and depreciation of currencies in terms of gold is purely a question of what should be the price of gold —a matter of great importance to producers of gold and to speculators in gold, but not for the question of trade between countries and the deficits or surpluses of international payments. It is as if the determination of the relative size of the yard and the meter would have to be expressed in terms of the cubit which was used in the building of the first temple in Jerusalem, even while the size of the cubit (the price of gold) is subject to negotiation!

Chapter 18

THE MYTH OF
"INTERNATIONAL MONEY"

WITH pegged exchange rates countries whose exports diminish or whose imports increase so that they find themselves with deficits, discover that they are "insufficiently liquid" internationally. They do not have enough "international money," which they identify with gold. Their shortage is really a shortage of foreign currencies to pay for the excess of imports over exports. This would be solved if they had more gold, which they would be able to sell for the foreign currencies they need. More dollars or more pounds, or indeed more diamonds, would also do the trick, but the historical hangup makes them express this in terms of gold as the original world money. This then takes the form of wide complaints that there is not enough international money altogether and leads logically to the conclusion that more international liquidity or international money needs to be created. This international money is said to be needed for carrying on the expanded volume of international trade just as in each country increased domestic money is needed for carrying expanded domestic trade. Furthermore, the complaint runs, while the need for increased domestic money has generally been met by governments in (at least) the required amounts ever since their "functional finance" escape from having domestic money limited by the supply of gold, this has not been done for international money (still identified with gold); and whoever put the gold into the hills did not adequately take into consideration how much would be needed for the growing needs of international money to finance the growing international trade.

There are two solutions to this apparent difficulty. One solution would be an increase in the quantity of gold. This is not possible. But there is a perfect substitute. While half a ton of steel is not a perfect substitute for a ton of steel, it happens to be the case that half an ounce of gold is able to perform all the *monetary* functions of an ounce of gold—(though not other functions like filling teeth) namely, to represent $35! Doubling the price of monetary gold is therefore exactly equivalent to doubling the supply of monetary gold and thereby doubling the quantity of "international money" held by the various countries, to the degree that they had stocks of gold. They would be able, with their gold stock, to acquire twice as much of the foreign currencies they need to pay for their import surpluses.

The other solution is to set up an international monetary authority (IMA) that would be able to create international money to the degree required, applying international functional finance in the same way that national monetary authorities apply functional finance in providing the money needed for domestic trade.

Unfortunately, both the problem of insufficient international money, and its solutions, all fall to the ground because it is a simple mistake to suppose that international trade requires an international money in the way that domestic trade in each country requires, and is supplied with, appropriate quantities of domestic money. There is no such international money used in international trade. *International trade is all done with domestic monies.* When French perfumes are imported into the U.S. they are paid for either in francs which the importer buys from the banks with dollars, or in dollars with which the French exporter buys from the banks the francs he needs to run his business in Paris.

It is possible that the talk of international money is connected with a simple semantic confusion stemming from the expression "international money market." This could give the impression of a market on which *international money* is traded. It is of course only an *international market* on which the different national monies are traded for each other.

The cry of insufficient international liquidity by the deficit countries really means insufficient foreign currency to maintain the pegging operation. It will be recognized as identical with the cry for help by any pegger of prices when he thinks that his *stock* is not quite large enough for the operation of his business and that he could be saved by temporary help—by a loan—when what he needs is a continuing subsidy to finance a continuing *flow* that he is absorbing. More gold would help only because it could be exchanged for foreign currencies. Any "international money" that might be created could be used only for precisely the same purpose, namely, to enable the deficit country to continue to enjoy the deficit, the acquisition of more imports than it can pay for out of the proceeds of its exports. The enjoyment of the deficit entails the sufferance of a surplus by other countries. These have to consent to continue exporting more than they import—in effect to work for the deficit country, producing exports for her to enjoy in return for nothing more than continually increasing stocks of IOU's. These IOU's may consist either of the money printed by the deficit country and acquired by the pegging, or any "international money" that would be created by an International Monetary Authority, or, what is also basically the same thing, increasing stocks of idle gold. In spite of many international monetary conferences, the unwillingness of surplus countries to keep on providing these subsidies to the deficit countries has prevented the establishment of an IMA with the power to create international money, until this was done on a minor scale in 1970 as we shall see in the next chapter.

Chapter 19

THE DOLLAR ABROAD:
II. How It Did Work

BY 1944, it had become sufficiently apparent that we were living in a changing world in which fixed exchanges could not be expected to stay fixed indefinitely.

It was therefore agreed, at Bretton Woods in that year, that the exchange rates then existing should no longer be quite so fixed. Every country was given the right freely to alter its exchange rate by as much as 10%, and the right to change it by more than that in the case of a "fundamental disequilibrium" which would have to be demonstrated to the IMF, the International Monetary Fund set up at that time. But this flexibility did not work. Deficit countries were reluctant to let their exchange rates move down, as if it were an affront to their prestige. Surplus countries resisted upward movements, partly because of their "sentimental internationalist" addiction to fixed exchange rates and partly because of objections by their exporters who would be hurt by the correction of the international balance of payments. They would no longer be able to sell the exports which the deficit country was paying for only with the borrowed money.

The most conspicuous demonstrations of the failure of Bretton Woods to bring about the necessary flexibility were the dollar shortage and the dollar glut. What was surprising was the ability of the fixed rates of exchange to last so long, from 1944 till 1971, with very few changes by the major trading countries. This was due to the dominant part played in international financial operations by the U.S. dollar.

The era of dollar scarcity was alleviated by the provision of a large supply of dollars to fill the gap in the form of foreign aid by the United States and in the form of massive gold purchases as the deficit countries gave up gold to finance their trade deficits. The era of the dollar glut was delayed for a very long time by a peculiar kind of readiness of the rest of the world to provide the U.S. with unprecedented loans. These were peculiar in that they were not considered as loans provided to help out a country running short of foreign exchange required for its pegging obligations. Rather, they were seen as the accumulation of reserves by the different countries, in dollars rather than in gold, against the day when they in turn might require massive quantities of foreign exchange to keep up the value of their own money if they should become deficit countries.

Alternatively, this could be looked upon not as a deficit but as the export by the United States of dollars as one of its export commodities, just like motor cars or tractors, or like the export of gold by the gold producing countries. The United States was able to keep on spending more abroad than it earned on its other exports because it was able to export dollars to the central banks (and to others) who wanted to accumulate stocks of dollars as contributions to their "international liquidity." There was not enough gold to supply the growing demand for *stocks* of international liquidity, large enough, it was hoped, to cover actual and feared future deficits created by the less and less appropriate fixed exchange rates. Dollars were therefore accumulated instead. The world had imperceptibly moved from a fixed exchange standard based on the gold content of the different currencies, to a fixed exchange standard based upon pegging the different currencies to the dollar.

The connection with gold was maintained only indirectly, by virtue of the United States's obligation to buy and sell gold at $35 an ounce. It had long ceased to be true that the value of the dollar, or of any other currency, was based on the value of gold. The value of gold was based on the readiness of the United States to buy gold at $35 an ounce and the readiness of speculators to buy and hoard gold in the hope that the United States would buy it back later at perhaps $70 or even $100 an ounce. Of course the price of gold could not rise above $35, no matter how optimistic the speculators were, as long as the central banks were freely selling gold at $35 an ounce, or the equivalent in other currencies at the fixed rate of exchange. But when the central bankers themselves began to share in this optimism and some obstacles were raised to the selling of gold by the central banks on the open market, the price of gold did rise on several occasions and in 1968 something was done about it.

In March 1968, in an apparent spat with speculators who had bid up the price of gold on the free market to some forty-odd dollars an ounce, the central banks decided to stop supplying such speculators with gold at $35 an ounce for them to resell at $41 or more (which they could not have done if the central banks had been keeping to their rule of selling unlimited amounts of gold at $35). In this fit of pique, they absent-mindedly also decided to stop *buying* gold from anybody except other central banks.

This meant that there were now two different kinds of gold! Monetary gold sold only by central banks to each other at $35 an ounce and non-monetary gold that could be freely traded at any price that cleared the market. This was called the two tier system. Since the price of gold had stayed at $35 an ounce since 1934 while almost everything else had gone up in price considerably during this period, many believed that central banks had been in a conspiracy to keep the price of gold down below some natural level. The opposite was nearer to the truth. It had been discovered that gold was not necessary for the manufacture of money, and all the other uses of gold took only about half the annual production of newly mined gold. The accumulated stock of gold had meanwhile grown to about a hundred times the annual industrial use. The "natural" price of gold, in the absence of its being hoarded by the central banks and by others, would be very much lower than the $35 per ounce at which gold was being pegged by the U.S. That the free price of gold was above $35 could only be due to the belief that the U.S. would raise the price it paid for gold, as was frequently rumored to be the intention.

The monetary gold, now to be used only for transactions between central banks, was thus turned into nothing but gigantic tokens, each ton of gold representing about a million dollars, to be moved like ponderous rings on a giant abacus to represent transactions between the central banks. It seemed that this would soon lead to a realization that a more convenient token would do just as well, even if it were made of plastic or ink marks on paper. The gold could then be set free for industrial uses and the end of the gold standard finally admitted officially. But this was not yet to be.

When speculators began to give up the hope that the U.S. would raise the price of gold, the price of gold on the free market began to fall. If it had fallen below $35 it might have collapsed the ancient myth that the long term price of gold can only move upwards and never downwards and so have contributed to the ending of the era of gold as international money the way it had already ended as domestic money. But when the price reached $35 and threatened to go below it, the central banks got cold feet and started buying gold again so as to prevent the price from falling below $35. This revived the hopes that the price would be raised to greater heights again sometime in the future.

At the same conference in March 1968, it was decided to issue "Special Drawing Rights" (SDR's) which were promptly dubbed "paper gold." This was not "golden paper" or paper that represented some gold stored somewhere. It was not "backed" by any gold anywhere, but was to be accepted as good as gold, or rather as good as the United States dollar, in its own right. This was seen by some as the beginning of truly international money, created by an international authority in the same way that national money is created by national monetary authorities. This, of course, had tremendous appeal to the sentimental internationalists. But there is very little to this dream. The quantity of SDR's was very small—some ten billion dollars to be created over three years, with most of this not available to the deficit countries. It had to be distributed in accordance with the different countries' shares in the International Monetary Fund, so that most of it went to the rich countries of which only the United States was in persistent deficit. It should be noted that the provision of additional credits to the United States was exactly what the conference was not in favor of. And finally, there is the fundamental difficulty that any large growth of such international money, if made available to the deficit countries, and these are the ones that complain about the insufficiency of international liquidity, could enable them to keep on enjoying their deficits only as long as the surplus countries were willing to keep on providing them with their unpaid-for imports.

Such a willingness of surplus countries to absorb "international money" was already gone *before* the SDR's were invented. The surplus countries—especially France—began to feel that they had already acquired too much "international money" in the form of United States dollars. Resentment at the extraordinary profitability of our business of exporting dollars added feelings of envy and antagonism, and the crisis developed. On August 15, 1971, President Nixon stopped the pegging of the dollar to gold or to other currencies and the dollar floated.

If nothing else had been done, the dollar would have floated down to the different levels in terms of different currencies, where the supply in each case would be equal to the demand. Nothing else would need to be done to solve once and for all the problems of dollar glut and of different degrees of shortage (or glut) of different currencies. The market in foreign exchange—the "international money market"—would have taken over the task that with fixed exchange rates is left to the nonexistent flexibility of money wages and prices.

The floating of the dollar implies the floating of other currencies in terms of the dollar, but in the opposite direction. Thus it seems impossible for the dollar (or any other currency) to be floated from one side only. The other countries, seeing the dollar float downward in terms of their currencies, would have to let their currencies float *upward,* in terms of the dollar.

This, however, would not matter to us at all once we had decided to maintain domestic prosperity without regard to what happened to our foreign exchange rate. All we need do is to *allow* the dollar to float by giving up *our* pegging activities. If other countries want to prevent the dollar from floating down, they can peg it themselves by buying up dollars with their

162

currencies whenever it shows any signs of falling. This enables us, indeed forces us, to keep on enjoying more imports. We can pay for these with the foreign currencies with which they are buying up our dollars, while we print additional dollars to take the place of those that they buy up and hoard or destroy. If they sell these dollars or use them, it defeats their purpose of keeping the value of the dollar from falling. And if we did not replace the dollars, we would be permitting them to inflict a domestic depression on us.

But this is not what we did. In December 1971, we agreed to fix the exchanges again at a new set of parities in terms of each other. These are almost certainly more appropriate to the present conditions than the rates fixed thirty or forty years ago. But with all the computerized mumbo-jumbo that went into the calculation and the negotiations, it is doubtful whether they will be able to stand for long because the world will go on changing. Already West Germany and Japan fear that the increase in the value of their currencies may constitute an over-valuation which will force them into depression and lead to a reconsideration of the whole setup. The growing recognition of the need for flexibility is shown by a much understressed novelty in the arrangements, namely, the provision of a much wider band within which the exchange rates are free to move— a span of 2¼% on either side of parity instead of the old 1%.

If the exchange rates are permitted to move freely in response to the market within the 4½% band allowed for by the new rules for pegging, the changing conditions of world trade and international monetary payments will bring some currencies up to the top of the band and others down to the bottom. The story then goes on just as before. There is, however, a possibility that the next logical step will be taken. This is to *move the band* in accordance with one of several possible rules. The band might move one or two per cent per annum, whenever the free movement of exchange rates reaches one edge of the band, in such a way as to permit the movement to continue. Alternatively, the band might be moved every three or six or twelve months, by having its center placed at the average rate of exchange during the preceding period.

If this worked smoothly for some time, people would realize that they had enjoyed the benefits of free exchanges. They would realize that the widened band and the crawling band (as the adjustable band has been called) are nothing but psychological aids, like water wings used by a beginning swimmer to give him confidence that he would not be pulled under the waves by a malignant sea-god, and which he will discard as soon as his confidence is established. This is perhaps the most likely way for the natural system of free exchanges ultimately to be established. The adoption of the wider band in 1971, and especially the lack of fuss about it, constitutes a very good omen.

There is, however, a considerable danger that history will be repeated and the permitted flexibilities will be disregarded, or rigidified, as were the flexibilities provided by the Bretton Woods agreements of 1944.

Appendix

THE DOLLAR STANDARD
or
HOW WE MISSED THE BOAT—*A Scenario*

What would have happened if we had let the dollar float freely not for four months but indefinitely—perhaps with a promise to reconsider the policy again after, say, four years?

One possibility is that the other countries (for this purpose represented by their central banks) would give up condemning us, on the one hand, for running a deficit and flooding the world with dollars—"exporting inflation"—and, on the other hand, for cutting off the supply of dollars required for "international liquidity." They would recognize that these complaints negate each other, get used to the floating currencies, and embrace the system of a free international money market.

They would then discover that they did not need their enormous hoards of gold and dollars, and they could not only enjoy the benefits of the international money market as it dissolved their deficits and surpluses and freed them to concentrate on domestic full employment and price stability, but as a special bonus they would be able to spend on useful goods and services the $40 billion or so they had accumulated.

They would, of course, be free to spend the dollars on any goods or services from any part of the world—including their own country. But in the last resort the goods and services would be provided by the United States. The dollars spent outside the United States would have to be traded in for the local currencies of the producers of such goods and services, and that would lower the price of the dollar in terms of these currencies. The dollar would have to fall to the level which, by cheapening our exports for them and making our imports relatively expensive for us, would increase our exports and reduce our imports to create the *surplus* in our balance of trade that would finance our repurchasing of our dollars. We would be paying back goods and services in return for the paper—the dollars—for which we had in the past been able to acquire goods and services from poorer countries. As the richest country in the world, we should hardly complain at having to give back the "foreign aid" we had somehow managed to get from the rest of the world.

This would be an eminently rational response by the rest of the world to our determination to let the dollar float. But what if the rest of the world did not want to go along with our "unilateral" decision that all countries should give up the game of pegging exchanges between crises? We have seen that although it takes agreement by *both* sides to have the rate of exchange between any two countries really free and unpegged, it is also possible to play the free exchange game *solitaire*. One country can just stop its pegging and get all the benefits of free exchanges *and more* by simply *allowing* its rate of exchange to float, paying no attention to what may be happening to the rate of exchange (as a result of its being pegged or otherwise traded in by others) and concentrating on maintaining domestic full employment without inflation, no matter what other countries said or did.

If the other countries did not want to accept freely floating exchange rates, they would endeavor to "maintain order" by continuing to peg "fixed" rates of exchange—either at the old rates or at some new set of parities (presumably arranged without our participation) at which they would peg their own currencies in terms of the dollar and in terms of each other. This would mean that although we had resigned from the pegging order, the dollar would still be pegged.

If they maintained the old parities, the U.S. deficit would of course continue. Furthermore, as we adopted policies to restore full employment, there would be a further increase in our imports and a further decrease in our exports as some exporters decided to use their resources for more profitable domestic production. The foreign countries would have to absorb the whole of this increased deficit, buying up and adding to their stocks of dollars this additional continuing supply. We would then be able to enjoy not only the output of our own full employment,

166

but an even greater excess of imports over exports than in the past for us to consume or invest.

We have been able to enjoy such deficits in the past because our dollars have been performing the same functions as gold. They were held as reserves for "international liquidity." At first, they merely supplemented the gold reserves, performing the function better than gold since they also yielded interest, and were more readily used for making payments when rumors began to circulate that the price of gold might be raised. Gold then began to lose some of its liquidity, since officially its price could not be raised prematurely, and its holders became more reluctant to pay it out. This increased still more the need for dollars as "international money."

If new parities were established, they might be such as would correct for the overvaluation of the dollar which was responsible for the "dollar glut." They would presumably be rates which were not expected to give rise to large deficits or surpluses —at least, initially. But they would not be likely to correct for the further U.S. deficits that would arise from our moving to full employment. Deficits would nevertheless develop, and there would be the same demand for increasing stocks of international money and a corresponding increase in demand for dollars for this purpose. This might turn out to be enough to cover our "full employment" deficit.

After things had settled down, we would begin to wonder why we were keeping our hoard of $10 billions' worth of gold now that we had retired from the pegging business, and we would decide to sell it for whatever it would bring. We would not be able to sell much of it at the high price on the free market ($46 an ounce on January 7, 1972) because the jump in the free market price can only be due to renewal of the hopes that we would return to pegging gold at a higher rate (on January 7, there was a remarkable rumor that we were going to raise the price to $140 an ounce). Our selling the gold would kill such speculation (reminiscent of the South Sea Cargo Cults). Unless the central banks bought up all the gold we sold, and none of them tried to dump their gold before the bottom fell out of the market, the price of gold would fall drastically, to perhaps $10 or $5 or less an ounce. Gold would completely cease to be of any use for international liquidity. It would become an ordinary metal like, say, aluminum, but one whose main use had disappeared while enormous stocks remain in existence, since it does not rust or decay.

With the final and complete demonetization of gold there would appear an enormous gap in the stock of "international money." Substitutes would be sought. An excellent substitute is readily available—U.S. dollars—which had already largely replaced gold and in effect had already become the international monetary standard. There would be a great increase in the demand for dollars to take the place of the ruined gold.

We might have some guilt feelings at having contributed to the annihilation of the greater part of the world's "international liquidity." We could happily make up for this by providing as many dollars as were demanded, either by selling them (buying and enjoying more imports and taking it easy in the production of exports) or by lending, or perhaps even giving away some billions of dollars—perhaps as aid to developing countries.

The resulting explicit dollar standard would work like a very much improved gold standard—one could say better than even an "ideal gold standard." An ideal gold standard is one by which no country would ever suffer from a deficiency of the supply of gold to provide the "international money" it needed. This would be the case if every country had a gold mine of a special kind from which it could take as much gold as it wanted

168

to at a constant cost in labor and resources of, say, the equivalent in its currency of $35 an ounce. The moment there occurred a deficit in any country's balance of payments, it could simply dig enough gold to pay it off at the established parity. With the dollar standard, it would always be possible for any country to acquire more dollars by producing more goods for the U.S. market. We would have to agree not to impose any restrictions or tariffs or quotas of any kind on our imports, so that with an insignificant reduction in price, deficit countries could increase their sales to us in what would look like enormous amounts to most countries, but would not seem very great to us. They could thus acquire additional dollars almost as they could acquire additional gold from the gold mines of the imaginary ideal gold standard.

Better still, the dollar standard, unlike even this ideal gold standard, would also work *in reverse*. A country finding itself with a *surplus* of gold could not throw the gold back into the gold mines, and have it magically return the resources spent in digging it out. With the dollar standard, they could. They could ship the surplus dollars to us and get in return all sorts of delightful items they could buy in the United States.

Any single country could, of course, spend any surplus gold in all the other countries on the gold standard, but any significant *general* surplus of gold would lead to a fall in the purchasing power of gold, either through inflation of prices relative to gold or through *revaluations* of their currencies by countries which did not want to accumulate "sterilized" gold surpluses.

We could prevent such a devaluation of the dollar, and at the same time raise the attractiveness of dollars as reserves of international liquidity, to heights never attained by gold itself. We could declare our intention of *stabilizing the value of the dollar*—not indeed in terms of gold, or even in terms of other currencies, but in terms of what dollars are ultimately good for, namely, for buying U.S. exports. We would want to stabilize our domestic price level for excellent domestic reasons. This would also normally give some stability to our export prices. However, we must recognize that we could conceivably fail to maintain domestic price stability, and even if we succeeded, our export prices could still rise.

What we could do is to *guarantee the purchasing power of the dollar in terms of our exports* as shown by an objective index number. The guarantee would take the form of an undertaking by our treasury to *compensate* any holder of dollars by giving him on, say, every Christmas day, as many additional dollars as might be needed to restore any such loss of purchasing power of the dollars he is holding. If our export prices had risen 5% in the course of the year, he would be presented with five cents for every U.S. dollar he owned.

The domestic repercussions of such a program are quite interesting. On the one hand, it would appear to be a tremendous responsibility and an additional very powerful reason for preventing inflation since that would involve obligations of perhaps billions of dollars to be paid out to foreigners as a free gift. It would strengthen policies designed to prevent inflation such as the incomes policy of Phase Two. On the other hand, it would have to be recognized that the compensation obligations would not really constitute any gift at all. It would merely mean our refraining from robbing the foreign and other holders of dollars through the decrease in the purchasing power of the dollar. It would only be giving back what had been filched from them in the increased prices of our exports, since buying these is the only thing the dollars are ultimately good for.

Both we and the rest of the world would benefit from this improvement over the gold standard as greater and greater quantities of the greatly improved "international money" came to be held by the central banks. Nevertheless countries would not remain happy. They would observe that we were making an enormous profit out of this arrangement, making the richest country of the world richer still. There would be attempts to muscle in on this bonanza—to persuade governments to keep other currencies as reserves instead of dollars, with perhaps even better and more attractive guarantees of possibly even greater future purchasing power or higher interest payments on the monies held. There would also be more direct competition in the creation of dollars by banks outside U.S. jurisdiction where they escape the normal reserve requirements.

This is indeed the nature of Euro-dollars. In a way, Euro-dollars look like real "international money," inasmuch as they are not any particular national money even though they are called dollars and are exchangeable dollar for dollar against U.S. dollars. It might equally be possible for banks in the U.S. to create "Americo-francs" not subject to the regulations to which French banks are subject, but there does not seem to be any demand to call forth such a supply, because the world is on a dollar standard—no matter what the French may say—and not on a franc standard.

Euro-dollars, rather than being international money, are better described as anarchistic money, or rootless cosmopolitan money, which serves to take the place of U.S. dollars only as long as they remain substitutable one for one against them. Being unregulated, they are subject to the same kind of over-expansion and possible runs and bankruptcies that overtook many national banks before they were regulated, guaranteed, and if necessary bailed out by their respective governments.

Such bankruptcies are not very likely since the art of banking has been very much developed since the old days, but if they should get into trouble it is not at all clear which central banks would think it their responsibility to bail them out.

To come back to the genuine U.S. dollar standard, its Achilles heel is that, like the gold standard and its successors that kept the gold standard's mantle, it is still a system of *pegged* rates, with its inevitable rigidity. There will be surplus countries and deficit countries and there will be much larger stocks of "international money" in dollars. But the surplus countries will tire of supporting the deficit countries and there will continue to be crises, depressions, devaluations, inflations, and revaluations in terms of the dollar. The discomforts and the resentments will all be turned against the U.S. which will continue raking in the profits from the expanding dollar reserves, calmly disdaining all these troubles abroad while maintaining price stability and full employment at home.

The resentment against the U.S., charging us with unpleasantnesses like "imperialism," "colonialism," "exploitation," would finally lead to the breakdown of the system. Either one by one, or possibly in groups, and conceivably even as a result of a joint decision, other countries would liberate themselves from this exploitation by cutting their connection with the dollar. This would mean letting their currencies float in terms of each other, as well as in terms of the dollar, which of course would mean finally letting the dollar float in terms of their currencies. They would then discover that the enormous reserves of dollars which they had acquired are no longer needed. This would be an enormous windfall. They would be able to use them for raising their immediate consumption levels or for increasing their investments. In short, they would be able to get us to pay back to them, in real goods and services, what they had been paying us in acquiring their dollar reserves. They would throw their dollars back into the magical dollar mine and get their investments back.

In this way there could ultimately be established a system of free exchanges for the whole world. We would no longer be able to carry on our extraordinarily profitable business of being the world's banker and providing the world's international liquidity of many billions, perhaps even hundreds of billions of dollars worth, at no significant cost, and we would have to return most of this profit when the dollars were returned to us, though we would still have benefited from the very large loans at low interest rates. This is one way in which we might ultimately bring about the benefits to all of free exchanges, even if the rest of the world would, for a very long time, prevent the dollar from really floating when we gave up pegging it. We could have got all these benefits and much more for a very long time if we had merely stopped caring about the prices of foreign currencies and of gold in terms of the dollar and set our boat free to float even if the others prevented it from really floating away. By giving in to the demand for a new set of fixed exchanges, we missed this chance.

A more likely route toward achieving free exchanges seems to be through the wider band of free exchange movement we have announced and the "crawling" of the band as the next logical step. Perhaps in a few years more rigidity will have set in and in a new crisis we may find ourselves with a similar opportunity.

The prophesied new crisis came much sooner than expected. In February 1973 there was another run on the dollar, but this time a general agreement could not be reached on a new set of exchange rates (such as was trumpeted just fourteen months earlier as "the most important international economic agreement in history"). While attempts continued to establish new "fixed" exchange rates between all the countries of the European Common Market, the dollar was left to float. This was due not to the success of economists in enlightening the politicians but to the failure of the negotiators to find a formula that would promise both fixity and flexibility of the exchange rates.

This development provides the U.S. with a second chance at the "Guaranteed Purchasing Power" (GPP) dollar standard described above. The floating dollar means that the U.S. can benefit from free, market-determined exchange rates, uncomplicated by the attempts of other countries to "protect" the dollar. There is no danger of gluts or of scarcities of the dollar as long as its price, in terms of other currencies, is free to move to the level where the supply is equal to the demand. At the same time the fixity of the European currencies in terms of each other provides a great and increasing need for "international money" as reserves against possible deficits. GPP dollars, provided by the U.S., are the ideal reserve, and this time, with the dollar freely floating, the European countries have no feelings of responsibility for "protecting" it which could explode into charges of American "imperialism." The massive liquidity provided by the GPP dollars can lubricate the trade of the European Common Market by filling the deficit-surplus gaps among its members, and it can do this much more efficiently than any artificial international money, like the SDR's. Such a GPP dollar standard, so useful to Europe and so profitable for the U.S., yet less provocative, could last until Europe adopted freely flexible exchange rates out of enlightenment rather than out of hostility to the U.S. or out of failure to refix exchange rates after some future exchange-rate crisis.

Chapter 20

PHASE FOUR:
INTERNATIONAL FUNCTIONAL
FINANCE

THE settlement of December 1971 was announced by President Nixon as the most significant monetary agreement in the history of the world. It was indeed the first time that such a complex set of new exchange rates was agreed to by so many countries. But it was essentially a lost opportunity. It was the second great lost opportunity of the New Economic Policy.

The first lost opportunity was the failure to restore the high employment which had been sacrificed in the pre-freeze mobilization of depression to fight inflation—the failure to establish the "instant prosperity" which the freeze had made possible. The second lost opportunity was the failure to continue floating the dollar indefinitely. This would ultimately have led all the large trading countries in the international economy to free their exchange rates as well from the rigidities which prevented the international money market from automatically balancing the balances of payments.

Our imposition of a 10% surcharge on import duties in August 1971 was basically a "persuader" to help Secretary Connally obtain agreement to a new set of fixed exchange rates which would correct the overvaluation of the dollar and restore the U.S.'s competitive position, and the surcharge was cancelled in December when this was achieved. But at some points in the negotiations, Secretary Connally declared that the U.S. could afford to let the dollar float indefinitely. Statements like this were presumably intended only as bargaining rhetoric, but even if said in jest they contain the profoundest truth.

Freeing the exchange rates of all the large trading nations would bring about the very objectives aimed at by those who resist such freedom of the exchanges in the name of some kind of international money, whether this were to be achieved by reverting to a genuine international gold standard or by setting up an international monetary authority which would establish some other kind of international money. Even if we reached a condition with domestic inflation beaten, with full employment no longer threatened by the resort to depression to fight inflation, and with wage and price regulation no longer needed to fight expectational inflation, there would still remain pressures on some countries to depart from full employment because of deficits in their balances of payments, for there will always be deficit countries and surplus countries. With free exchanges this problem is taken care of too.

Free exchanges may thus be considered the true international functional finance. While national functional finance includes a national monetary authority to provide the proper quantity of national money, it is a mistake to apply this analogy to the international economy. Basically this is because the international economy does not make use of international money. It cannot make use of international money because the conditions which would make international money work— as in the idealized gold standard—do not exist. The necessary conditions for international money to work can take one of three forms:

(1) Legally free, culturally acceptable and economically practical mobility of people from relatively depressed parts of the world (from which international money has been moving) to the relatively more prosperous parts of the world (into which international money has been moving—that is why they have become depressed or prosperous). It is precisely such mobility within a country that makes it possible for the different parts of the country to enjoy a single currency. In the same way, a group of countries that are very closely tied to each other, economically, culturally and politically, could enjoy fixed exchange rates among the currencies in the group. Economically speaking, they constitute a single country.

(2) Such flexibility of wages and prices that the changes generated in relative price levels (by movements of international money from one country to another) are sufficient to increase sales from the deficit countries and to increase purchases by the surplus countries in a sufficient degree to dissolve the deficits and surpluses.

(3) Some arrangements whereby appropriately different rates of inflation in the different countries are brought about that will be just right to correct the balance of payments. This means sufficiently greater inflation in the surplus countries as compared with inflation in the deficit countries to bring about the required equalization of imports to exports.

The nonexistence of any of these conditions leaves only adjustments in rates of exchange among the currencies of different countries (or among groups of economically integrated countries) to dissolve deficits and surpluses, although pegging can fill the gap as long as surplus countries are willing to provide credit or gifts to deficit countries.

Groups of countries which are not so closely integrated can benefit very greatly by establishing customs unions or free trade areas which would enable them to gain from increased trade and the efficiencies of greater degrees of specialization. For this it is necessary to reduce or abolish restrictions on trade, on capital movements and on the movement of workers and businessmen among countries. It is, however, not necessary for them to have fixed exchange rates among their currencies any more than for them to have a single monetary unit. On the contrary, attempts to maintain fixed rates of exchange among different countries in an economic union result in deficits and surpluses among the countries which, if they are not corrected by adjustments in the exchange rates, will establish pressures for restrictions that would break up the economic union. Nevertheless, members of an economic union generally have an even stronger attachment to fixed exchange rates among their constituent countries than do the members of the world community as a whole. It's a kind of "sentimental Europeanism" (in the case of the European Economic Community) that breeds the same kind of harm out of good intentions as does "sentimental internationalism."

International functional finance, in the form of free flexibility of the exchanges, with no attempts at pegging, would thus complete the structure of the New Economic Policy and would bring to the whole world the possibility of full employment policies with neither inflation nor depression. This we may call Phase Four.

In the rest of this chapter we will consider some of the objections to and some other implications of a system of

International Functional Finance—a system of freely floating exchanges.

First there is the tendency to suppose that free exchanges would mean wildly fluctuating exchanges. This is probably due to free exchanges having been observed only for very short periods when a pegging system has broken down and the natural level of the exchanges is far from the pegged rates and has to be discovered by trial and error. Nevertheless, whenever exchanges have been free for any significant period they have almost always quickly settled down—except where violent domestic inflations were going on and the rates of exchange had to adjust to the changing domestic price level. In such cases the "fixed" rates of exchange also have to be changed very frequently too. Thus Brazil, with inflation going on at 20% a year and more, has a "fixed" rate of exchange that is changed about once a month.

The period between August 15, 1971, and December 22, 1971, is perhaps not a very good example to use because there was so much political, as well as economic, speculation going on. But everybody was surprised at the orderliness of the "floats" that took place. The eagerness of the European and Japanese central banks to get a new set of "fixed" exchange rates may well have been due not so much to their fear of the free exchanges not working, as to a fear that they might already be working only too well—so well as to generate doubts as to whether central bankers are really necessary for international monetary management. (Read: pegging the rates of exchange.)

A common bogey is that in the absence of an orderly (read: pegged) exchange system, there would be a danger of "competitive devaluation." As long as the exchanges are being pegged, devaluation is shunned as a fate worse than death. When it is finally forced on a country, it is usually greeted as liberation. The fear of competitive devaluation is presumably a fear that excessive jubilation at the liberation will create an urge for more of the same. Once devaluation releases a country from an overvaluation of its currency so that its increased competitiveness dissolves its balance of payments deficit, it may want to devalue still further, for still greater competitiveness, to be rewarded by a *surplus* in its balance of payments. But the surplus of one country is always the deficit of other countries and the other countries will want to devalue, competitively, to cure their deficits, and perhaps even to attain surpluses themselves. This is the competitive devaluation bogey, which is said to await us if we depart from an "orderly system"— i.e., a system of pegged exchange rates.

Again it is the habit of thinking of gold that gives rise to confusion. Competitive devaluation is possible if it is conceived of as competitively bidding up the price of gold. This may make gold very expensive, depending on the supply by producers and the holders of gold as its price is bid up. But what is significant is not the price of gold, but the rates of exchange. Country A, if it is not satisfied with the equilibrium value of its currency in terms of Country B's currency, as reached by supply and demand on the international money market, *can* lower its value in terms of B's currency.

The way to do this is to bid up B's currency in terms of its own, by buying up and holding on to, as much of it as is required. If Country B doesn't like the resulting appreciation of its currency (which reduces *its* competitiveness in international trade) it can do exactly the same—print unlimited quantities of B money with which to buy up A money and bid up its price. The two activities cancel each other. Nothing is changed except a boom in the money printing industry in both countries. It is to be expected that the fruitlessness of buying up, even costlessly, another country's money, which that country can supply costlessly, would quickly lead everyone concerned to stop spinning wheels this way, even if they ever started—nor would it matter significantly if they continued.

What makes competitive devaluation look rather frightening is the similarity of its symmetry to that of other deficit-reducing devices that really *are* damaging. Restrictions on imports may be imposed to improve the balance of payments, although generally this is done not when free exchanges dissolve deficits and surpluses, but where a country is running out of foreign currency reserves (and credits) but feels that it must continue pegging its exchange rate. Retaliatory tariffs and quotas and other restrictions may ensue. Unlike "competitive devaluation" this actually happens, and when it does, only the effects on the balance of payments cancel out and the restrictions on trade remain, hurting both countries in a genuine "beggar-thy-neighbor" process of economic warfare.*

---

* There is another argument often raised against free exchanges that is rather technical, but I am tempted to mention it here because it consists of a theorem I wrote about almost forty years ago which has somehow become known as the Lerner-Marshall condition. This is the condition under which the automatic depreciation of a currency, caused by a deficit in the balance of payments, would not cure the deficit but make it worse. If the cheapening of a country's exports increased its sales in a smaller proportion than the price reduction, the total revenue in foreign currency would be less than before. If, at the same time, the increased cost of imports reduced the imports very little, the reduction in the value of the imports might be less than the reduction in the value of the exports, so that the import surplus is increased, and the balance of payments would have worsened.

I have always considered this as of practical significance only in some very exceptional cases because there are so many different kinds of actual and potential imports and exports that it is hard to imagine such very tiny reactions to a depreciation. But if the condition should nevertheless arise, there is also, as I pointed out at that time, a remarkable antidote.

In the course of many lectures on the subject of this book, I have often been condemned for not dealing with all sorts of other evils in our society, evils which would not be cured by even the most complete achievement of Phase Four. Indeed because I thought it irrelevant to come out against such evils, I have even been accused now and then of being in favor of them. Yet when I consider what social ills *would* be alleviated, if not cured, by the policies considered in this book, by national and international functional finance and the avoidance of administered inflation and depression, I am almost scared by the wide spectrum that is covered.

I have mentioned the injustices of inflation for unfortunates with relatively fixed small incomes. I have only hinted at the damage done to the efficiency of the economy when all prices are rising so rapidly that one cannot see the *relative* price changes which guide the management of the economy. But much more serious than these are the evils from depression, whether "natural" or "administered." The list of social evils

---

If a country should find itself in this queer fix, where the automatic depreciation of its currency only makes the deficit worse, the cure is to arrange the opposite—an appreciation!

The country should borrow a large sum of foreign money. It should have no difficulty because it could show that it would easily be able to pay it back. It should use this foreign money to buy up its own currency on the international money market, bringing about an appreciation of its currency. Given the tiny responses of the Lerner-Marshall condition, the increased price of its exports would reduce sales very little so that there would be a large increase in foreign money earned. The decreased domestic price of imports would cause only a tiny increase in imports so that there would be very little more foreign money required to pay for them. The net increase in foreign money would become available for paying off the foreign money loan and there would be the further continuing gain from being able to enjoy more imported goods and having to make fewer exports. It seems a pity that a disease that could be cured by such a delightful remedy should be so rare.

which are aggravated by depression and unemployment sound almost like a complete list of all the ills imaginable.

Where there are not enough jobs to go around, it is inevitable that employers will look for ways to make life easier by leaving out of consideration many groups of people who are clamoring for the inadequate number of jobs available. This leads to discrimination—by race, by sex, by age, and by any other distinguishing mark which would enable an employer to cut down the great number of applicants that he must see for a very few jobs. In a depression there is no need for employers to be much concerned about the happiness, welfare, or convenience of their employees. All their attention is concentrated on trying to obtain more customers. With high employment, this would be reversed. In a depression, while the unemployed generally suffer more than businessmen do, profits fall more than wages. Wages never become negative. The fear of negative profits, or losses, will induce firms to try to save themselves by forming monopolies. Envy and crime increase when people find themselves left out of the economy and see others do well when they are doing so badly.

On the international field there are parallels to this. Where countries, for whatever reason, feel that it is dangerous, illegitimate, improper, or for any other reason impermissible to allow a deficit in their balance of payments to be corrected by the automatic adjustment of depreciation of their currency, they have to engage in other measures for dealing with the deficit. They will be pushed into domestic depression. To ameliorate that, they will turn to genuine "beggar-thy-neighbor" policies, in trying to export their unemployment to other countries by restricting imports, by limiting capital exports, by pursuading their citizens to buy domestically rather than abroad, and by imposing exchange controls. Where there are agreements against such restrictions, these will be subverted under the guise of health regulations and other subterfuges.

To some countries the restrictions on their exports might seem a minor issue, but it can be a matter of life and death for countries with urgent needs for imports which can be paid for only by the money earned from a limited number of possible exports. Such countries will fear their whole lives imperiled and may even be induced to resort to war. I do not think this is the most important danger of war nowadays, but it is a significant contribution.

In discussing inflation, deflation, and balance of payments problems, we must abstract from many other ills. But if we are successful in dealing with these problems, we will be removing the *basic* sickness, which is unemployment. The importance of the other problems lies primarily in that they can bring about unemployment. And what looked like a large number of independent ills are merely the numerous symptoms of the basic sickness.